Always the Victor, Never the Victim

Ashley N. Skelton

Dedicated to my Dad, Gregory Gibson, who didn't live long enough to see this dream come to life. Also dedicated to my amazing husband Eli who has supported me for the last eleven years, and our four beautiful children Noah, Cailey, Reagan, and Little Eli.

Acknowledgement

The experience of writing this book has been both hard and humbling. I could not have done this without the help of my husband Eli, who spent hours editing for me. I am truly thankful for not only his help, but also his support through this entire process.

I want to thank Kerry-Ann who has been such an amazing guide and mentor throughout this whole process. Steering me constantly in the direction that I needed to go to make this happen. Rachel Dolcine I owe a huge thank you to for being a great mentor and friend.

I couldn't have done this without my best friend Courtney, she encouraged me and cheered me on every single day. She gave me the courage to keep writing even on the hard days. Courtney has been a massive cheerleader in my life and someone I'm honored to call a friend.

The Billings Gazette was wonderful in taking the time to talk to me and granting me permission to use a news article written by them. Also Cobb County court system, they are truly rockstars of record keeping, allowing me to have the legal documents needed to tell my story.

I am truly thankful for the people God used in my life to help me get to this point. I owe Dr. Killebrew the biggest hug ever for her kindness. Luci Hough has been a huge blessing to my life, and I could never thank her enough for her guidance at a hard time in my life.

I would also like to thank Jake Schmidt, for doing what he does and being a friend over the years. He is someone that truly does a thankless job and deserves all the recognition for his efforts.

Thank you to my dad Gregory Gibson, for trying everything he could to protect me. I wish dad was here to see this book become real, as I know he would be so damn proud.

I could go on for pages and pages thanking my counselor Ann-marie, detectives, and agents who took the time to try to help me and they all deserve credit for where I am today.

Thank you to everyone who reads this book; you don't know what it means to me.

Mostly, I want to thank God. I am where I am today because of His never-ending love and salvation through His Son, Jesus Christ..

Warning

Grab a trash can or a barf bag before reading, you're going to need it. The events of this book are true and very real. This is MY story. I included this warning to both advise and protect the reader from anything that could be potentially triggering. This book includes taboo topics not often discussed such as rape, incest, kidnapping, physical, mental, verbal and sexual abuse. Some names will be changed in order to maintain respect of privacy and names have been redacted from news articles and legal documents as well. This book should not be taken lightly.

Introduction

The click of the lock and the sound of the door opening, while still in the foggy haze between being completely asleep and half-awake, brought back the fear of being 14 years old again...and my first abuser entering my room. Fear began to creep in. Who was coming through the door?

My body was not awake enough yet to know, but somehow my mind and the demons of my adolescent self knew to be on high alert. Footsteps echoed through the house, sounding heavy against the hardwood floors. So heavy that even the sound of the fan couldn't drown them out. My heart was racing faster. Although, not completely alert yet, I was scared.

The house was dark and seeing someone would be nearly impossible. What if I needed to fight? What if they had a weapon? Would they kill me? These thoughts ran rampant as I started to awaken more, but I didn't dare move from my spot in the bed. My dog started to growl a low, deep, and vicious growl preparing to defend me at all costs. I caught a glimpse of the shadow and watched it dance across the living room wall. Although the house was dark, the small and very light amber lamp kept on the table in the living room allowed me to see the shadow slowly moving across the way. The sound of the footsteps was growing louder as they got closer to my room. The thumping of my heart could be heard for miles or so it seemed. I just knew whoever it was would find me. I was fully awake now.

Reaching for my phone wasn't an option, they might see my movement and come for me. The silhouette of a man appeared in the doorway. The backlighting made it hard to make out his features. I could tell it was a large man, broad throughout the chest and shoulders with large strong arms, becoming slimmer at the waist almost in the shape of a "V". He stepped into the doorway of the bedroom and the light from the TV caught the ginger beard and ball-cap he wore.

It was my husband, who should have been home hours ago, but got held up at work. I wish I could tell you that we laughed at my anxiety-stricken fear, and both went to bed without any care in the world, but that's not how things work for me. I fear the sounds of locks, doors, and footsteps in the night.

***

I can't promise this book will resonate with everyone or that it will help you, but what I can promise is it will be raw, real, and full of taboo topics. Talking about fears such as depression, anxiety, and PTSD are not your run-of-the-mill dinner conversations, but are absolutely real in my world and in the lives of so many people today.

My hope is that my story reaches someone. It may be the 14-year-old suffering depression, it may be the 20-year-old trying to maneuver life after sexual assault. Perhaps it resonates with the woman who put her baby up for adoption and is living life with the "what-if" scenario in the back of her mind.

I'll be painting pictures that not everyone can easily digest. After all, this is my true authentic self. My story, my struggles, my defeats, and my victories. It's the story of how I went from victim to victor.

According to researchers, 1 out of 4 girls and 1 out of 13 boys will experience sexual abuse before the age of 18[1]. Of those children, 90% will be sexually abused by someone the child or child's family knows[2]. That is a startling statistic, because we all know someone, whether they have come forward or not, that has been sexually abused as a child. It is a statistical certainty.

I believe with such a high number of sexual assaults in both children and adults, these incidents are the catalysts for anxiety, depression, PTSD, and suicides we see in adults today. Some child victims find themselves trying to escape a reality that can't be escaped, thereby turning to substance abuse, alcohol, a life of crime, or worst of all, becoming the very abuser they hated so much.

---

(1) Pereda, N., Guilera, G., Forns, M., & Gomez-Benito, J. (2009). The prevalence of child sexual abuse in community abd student samples: A meta-analysis. *Clinical Psychology Review, 29*, 328-338. doi:10.1016/j.cpr.2009.02.007

(2) Finkelhor, D., & Shattuck, A. (2012). Characteristics of crimes against juveniles. Durham, NH: Crimes Against Children Research.

As a child victim myself, I won't lie to you and tell you that life has always been great, and my world is full of fairy-glitter and smiles. I get up every day and continue to keep swinging. I found God in the journey to my authentic self, and He has used me in such powerful ways and is continuing to do so. I say I found God, he was always there, I just didn't know it. He didn't need to find me. He was with me the entire way. He gave me a story to tell and now He's given me the task of telling it.

Chapter 1

The Genetic Jackpot

My birth didn't result in some grand genetic jackpot. I was born to probably two of the most selfish and self-centered people I personally know. Mix the two together and you have the ultimate recipe for disaster. But somehow in both the throes of lust and a tumultuous marriage, almost exactly ten months after they were married, I entered this world. I was born on a crisp, cool morning in October, innocent to life's plans ahead. Both of my biological parents are far too self-centered to really have children at all, but I guess in some weird way, I owe them both a thank you for lying down in the heat of passion, thus creating my brother and I. Even though neither one of them should be parents, I am here and there was indeed a plan for me and a story to tell. You know the saying, "Life dealt me a bad hand"? It dealt me a bad everything, up to a certain point in my life. My life was filled with men entering and exiting my biological mom's (we'll call her Stacy) life, and women doing the same with my biological dad (we'll call him Stan). It was like a Greyhound bus station: just as one pulled away, another entered.

Some of those men and women were nice. The nice ones often didn't stick around long as they saw exactly the people my biological parents were, which were liars, cheaters, users, abusers and manipulators. Although to hear my Stacy tell it, my brother and I were the reason those relationships didn't work out.

My brother and I were pieces of their puzzle, waiting to be moved into the places we fit. We were being lied to, beaten, or dragged to the next house, apartment, town, or even state. Our "biologicals" refused to co-parent. They were too busy talking badly about one another when we were around either of them. This ultimately made it impossible to enjoy time with either "parent" and made me feel guilty for loving the other.

Our safe space was with our grandparents. Our grandparents, Stan's parents, allowed us to visit often and they taught us a lot. I was personally taught firearm safety and how to use a firearm by my Pop and Grandma. Those are moments I enjoyed as a child. I know Stacy had jobs and worked, but she never missed going on a date or taking a vacation without us.

My other grandparents, Stacy's parents, made me learn my multiplication tables. It's laughable now, but I was so mad at having to spend my vacation learning, but I now understand their intentions. Although, I think I remember Stacy teaching me the magic of flashcards for studying. Beyond that, I don't recall anything else.

Stan was just as bad. I can't recall a single thing Stan taught me. He was cocky and vain, almost to the point of annoyance, thinking he was better than everyone else. He would belittle people with extra weight, or messed up teeth and feet, or anyone he found unattractive. The biggest issue was that Stan tended to "sleep around" and traded-in women like cars. It was a constant struggle to adapt to someone new.

We had no stability in life. It was always someone new. I don't know how many times Stan has been married to this day, mainly because I've lost count. Oftentimes while visiting my Pop and Grandma, he would call and promise to visit, only to leave me and my younger brother staring out their window for hours, anticipating his arrival...closely watching for a "dad" that never showed. These weren't isolated incidents, they were our normal.

We learned to be disappointed when it came to our "parents" very early in life. This didn't even include the atrocities we experienced: witnessing someone being shot just feet away, being forced into a locking trunk full of Legos by Stacy's boyfriend's son, being hit so badly with belts that it left bruises for days or even weeks, or being left on the side of the road by Stacy's boyfriend at about six years old, with your little brother - only four years old - in tow. We were destined for hardship because both of our bios were selfish and cared only about what they wanted, not the mental or emotional needs of their children.

Chapter 2

Cash Cow

Around the age of four, I personally started getting a little more attention from Stacy, as she discovered I was quite a talented singer. From that point on, I sang. When I started singing, I loved every minute of it. I was good at it, and it gave me positive attention. In fact, it's the only positive attention I'd ever gotten. However, I was raised in bars with drunk adults everywhere, because "that's where I would get discovered" according to Stacy. Most kids between the ages of 5 or 6 to around 12 or 14 get to go outside, hang out with their friends, ride bikes, and just be kids.

Not this girl…a show was coming up or karaoke was the next night and I needed to practice. I'd spend hours a day practicing with Stacy sitting in front of me giving tips, tricks, and lessons, thinking she knew exactly what I needed to do. For shows, I had fancy outfits and frilly dresses, while my brother was tossed a Nintendo

Gameboy and told to go to his room. Some nights I wouldn't get back to the house any earlier than 1 or 2 AM from singing and had to be up for school in just a few hours. I competed regularly for concert tickets, cash prizes, you name it, I did it.

At one particular competition, the stage coordinators were having trouble with my music, and I got nervous and froze. I didn't place in that final round and Stacy was pissed that I "just stood there." She was completely unrealistic about the fact that I was the one on stage and she was in the audience. It takes a lot of courage to put yourself on a stage for people to mock or criticize you, but that's something she'll never understand.

Shortly after that, I somehow got coerced into singing for my orthodontist. A man with a recording studio heard me from the waiting room and started setting up appointments with Stacy. For me, it started out as being exciting because in my mind, "Oh my goodness, a record studio…this could be my big break." I quickly found out how the "music industry" works. I had a love for country and old rock music. It was what I was passionate about. I got *told* I would produce a Christian album. Now, I have nothing against Gospel music, actually I love it, but it was not what I wanted to sing at the time. However, I was convinced that this album would allow me to "break-in to Nashville" or big record companies. So, I signed the contract. I was young, dumb, and chasing a dream. I did what I thought might get me there, or at least what I was told would get me there. I was forced to record under circumstances in which studio time should have been rescheduled.

As a kid, I used to break out in cold sores. In one instance my entire top lip was covered in them and was swollen. I looked like someone had punched me in the mouth. I begged Stacy to let me stay home from school which she did, but we couldn't miss studio time. I was forced to go and sing. The Gospel album that was produced is ok, but if I had more control over the days that I was sick or wasn't singing well, it could have been so much better. I wasn't given that choice.

Stan had NEVER heard me sing before that CD was released. I started singing at four years old, and the CD was produced when I was around twelve. I've even been coerced to perform outside Stacy's job at Red Lobster with a tip bucket at the front of my "stage", which was basically the tacky deck that Red Lobster used to have. I used to love to sing but it became a job.

Being forced took all the joy of singing away for me. I never got compliments from either "parent", except for when I was singing. I was exposed to bars, smoky honky-tonks, and drunk, grown men who "cat-called" ladies.

I didn't have a standard, set bedtime. I didn't have a typical childhood because Stacy saw me as a way to get in with a record company. I was young and believed I had talent, I wasn't the best in my opinion, but I had potential. At this time, teen acts and performers were all the rage. She saw dollar signs and a meal ticket. But unfortunately for her, this heifer didn't produce the cash.

I continued to sing on my own in karaoke places but only for fun and to keep what little bit of love for music I had going. Since this time, my goals and dreams have changed, and it has left me with a sense of self-awareness. I can love music and I can love to sing while cleaning my kitchen, or dancing around the house like the idiot I am. It doesn't have to be monetized in order to bring me joy. It can just be something I genuinely love to do.

Chapter 3

The First Mistake of Many

Around the age of thirteen, Stan, for whatever reason, decided I could be around him more. I don't know why since I was nothing more than a Cinderella-style babysitter. Responsibility for all of the younger kids in the house, which included a newborn at one point, fell upon my shoulders. I was liable for keeping up with them while Stan and his girl slept because they worked overnight in clubs. I cooked, changed diapers, you name it, I did it. I was a parent to kids that didn't even belong to me.

I remember the house vividly. Entering the two glass-paneled doors, was a wide-open area where the living room and kitchen were only divided by a wall. To the left was a laundry room and a big room with steps. For a while, that room acted as a living room or an entertainment room where we'd watch movies, and the younger boys would rough house. To the right, and down a longer hallway, were three bedrooms. One was a master bedroom with a bathroom and the other two rooms were smaller, kid rooms. One belonged to my younger brother,who lived with Stan at the time, the other belonged to the two little girls whose mom was married to Stan. I didn't live there, I visited on school breaks and during summer vacation.

Things changed like the wind around that place. At the time, the woman he was married to was more interested in being a friend to us instead of a parent. Her idea of "parenting" was teaching me how to "twerk".

I vividly remember being cursed and yelled at because I overslept, and the younger kids got up and painted the big screen TV with peanut butter and had stuff everywhere. Apparently, I was the adult in the house. If dysfunctional was a family, it was ours. Honestly though, I never made a big deal about it because I loved all the kids and what good would it do anyway to fuss about it? My younger brothers did stupid stuff and it kept things interesting, to say the least.

Eventually, the living and entertainment room became the master bedroom. I guess it gave the adults a bigger room. I can't remember the exact date, as it's all a fog now, but I do remember lying in Stan's bed watching a movie with him and some of my brothers. My brothers eventually got tired, got up, and went to their beds. Stan and I laid there watching the movie, and at some point, I guess we both fell asleep.

I woke up with Stan's hand down my shorts, touching me, and trying to take my shorts off. He claims he was asleep and didn't mean to. I was scared and didn't know what to say. How do you react to that? I was thirteen years old, scared, embarrassed, and didn't know what to do.

I had never been touched in any way before, my brain went into paralysis. I didn't cry. I think I was in too much shock. He lit a cigarette and sat on the steps shaking as if he couldn't believe that had just happened. This was the start of what would become two years of hell for me.

The next day, he called me to the room and locked the door. He pushed me onto the bed and tongue-kissed me - I froze. I didn't cry, I didn't say no. I just froze. I didn't know what to do except look at the ceiling and count the cracks on it. That became my escape, counting cracks on the ceiling. He pulled my pants off. Lowered his pants just enough to expose himself. He spat on his hand and rubbed it on me and himself and then he penetrated me. I lost my virginity to incest. I'll never forget the words he leaned down and whispered in my ear, "I just popped your cherry".

The whole thing probably lasted five minutes. I honestly don't remember, it seemed like forever and time stood still in those moments. When he was done, he pulled himself out and ejaculated on my stomach. I pulled up my shorts and ran to the bathroom to clean up. I was bleeding. I started a shower, locked the door, and sat in the bathroom, crying. I had no one to tell, I had no one I thought would believe me. For two years, I suffered in silence. This was the first of many assaults by my own biological father.

The assaults became more frequent. It also became a way to barter and trade for things. If I asked him for money for whatever, it came at a price. It could be as simple as using my hands to touch him or it could be as severe as rape or oral "favors." I didn't put up much of a fight when it came to him wanting something in return when I asked for money to go to the mall or to the movies because he was going to do it anyway. Why would I make things harder for myself? I did things that would utterly disgust me, just to be able to get time away from him. These instances would later lead me to have issues with my own sexuality and my own intimate relationship with my husband.

The assaults became more frequent, as did my counting of the cracks in the ceiling. I've always wondered how no one could tell, especially his wives or girlfriends. Did they honestly have no clue? Was he that good at hiding it? Was I that good at appearing normal? Or did they just not care? I felt like no one saw me. I was invisible to the world around me. I was so embarrassed by the things I was forced or coerced to do, that lying became second nature to me. I didn't want to face the facts. I didn't want to believe that I had lost my virginity to Stan. The thought alone, or even typing it now, turns my stomach.

I'd reluctantly faced the fact that I was damaged goods. I was shattered pottery that had been demolished and the pieces would slowly be put back together. It's hard to relive those moments. I hear words he said to me, and they make me sick and drive my anxiety through the roof.

I remember during one of my assaults, he asked me, as he penetrated me yet again, "what if I never get tired of this…what if I always want you?" Please take this time to run to the bathroom and vomit, I know I have. I prayed at that moment for him to please get tired of me, get tired of this, or for someone to please catch him. It never happened and the suffering just continued.

Mind-tricks were played constantly. One day, I threatened to tell. He called my bluff. I wanted to cry out so badly, but the shame and disgust I felt for myself was like stuffing an old dirty sock in your mouth and sealing it with duct tape. You just choke it down to avoid having to admit it, even to yourself. He said, "If I'm sick enough to do it, I'm sick enough to go down for it." It was not the answer I wanted; my hope was that the threat would have been enough to stop him, but nothing ever did. So, I continued to count cracks.

Chapter 4

Grooming

A year after Stan started molesting me, a guy, who we'll call "Rob", started hanging out at the house. He was cool in my eyes. And really into music like I was, so we could talk music for hours. Rob taught me about several different bands and new music. He was very tall, around six-foot five inches, and thin with light red hair and crystal blue eyes. He was someone I thought of as a "friend."

Rob started to come around more and more and when he wasn't around, we chatted online in a private chat room. Mistake number two. Chat rooms are filled with predators, who know exactly what to say to coerce young, vulnerable girls and boys. Chat rooms were my undoing. I didn't understand the dangers of chat rooms. I was a 90's kid, so "stranger danger" was the creepy guy in the store, the weird white van in the neighborhood, or a neighbor you steered clear of.

Chat rooms were a whole new portal into a world of grooming and being coerced into dangerous, real-world situations. According to Childrescuecoalition.org, up to 85% of online predators are hands-on abusers of children. Rob made me believe I could trust him. I didn't trust most people in my life because of my experiences. I was too scared to tell the few people I did trust, like my Pop and Grandma. Sexual assault of any magnitude can leave one fearful, untrusting, and anxious. Depression sets in, and the things you are forced to do or are coerced into doing becomes robotic in a sense.

Rob seemed different to me. He really seemed to care. He listened and talked to me. Having experienced very little attention, other than the abuse, I fell for his trap. I remember it like it was yesterday because some things are just seared into the mind. Rob was over at Stan's house for New Year's Eve. Everyone was hanging out and watching TV. We all rang in the New Year and had a great time. The adults went to bed. Rob was told to stay because it was late and people who had been drinking would be out. So, he parked himself on the couch.

I remember sitting on the couch with him watching a movie. I asked if he minded if I laid my head on his lap. He said sure. I felt like I trusted him more than other people, after all that's what groomers do. They make you feel safe, wanted, and even "loved." So, when he slipped a hand into my pants and started to rub on me, I was aroused. I'm ashamed to say I was enjoying it, but I thought he loved and cared about me. Becoming aroused is a natural reaction when you think the person cares. Due to the skewed situation with Stan, I thought grown men wanting a young girl was also normal.

Rob took his time with me. He was not rough, nor did he try to hurt me like Stan had. For the first time, I experienced what I thought was love. Rob asked me if I was a virgin. For the record, predators love virgins. It's like a prize or a trophy to them. It also makes it easier to manipulate their victims. If they are your first sexual experience or first "love", the manipulation tactics and gaslighting are endless. I told him yes out of embarrassment, mainly because who wants to tell anyone that they lost their virginity to a biological parent: that's the ultimate shame.

The answer appeased him at the moment, but later on down the road he told me he knew I was a liar. He said he knew what a popped cherry feels like, that he had taken his fair share of virgins, and that I definitely wasn't one. It was like he was bragging about them and embarrassing me at the exact same time.

Another red flag for a predator, they love to feel powerful and to make their victim feel powerless. Still, I didn't tell him it was Stan. That was something I kept close to my heart for 2 years. It was too much to acknowledge it myself sometimes. In my mind I was garbage, not worthy of anything, so who cared what I did? More importantly, I had just started a vicious cycle for myself that was going to take an act of God to break, and He would (eventually) break those chains I carried but not before I was willing. Then things got even tougher.

Chapter 5

The Hotel

New Year's Day came and went. I continued talking to Rob daily. I had a school project to do: going to work with someone to observe what they did for a living. Well, I clearly couldn't go with Stan or any of his girlfriends. They were all working in the club scene, and I was only 14 years old. This gave me an excuse to go hang out with Rob. He was a maintenance man for a hotel. Stan agreed to let me go and spend the day at work with him.

The hotel was nice, with green carpeting, lined by fresh, white walls. I got to the hotel at the beginning of Rob's shift. Due to him being a maintenance man, he had a master key card to any and all rooms in the hotel. He immediately found a room we could hang out in until he got called so that "the customers couldn't see me." I'm not sure if that was an excuse or if his management told him I couldn't go into customer rooms with him to see what he actually did for work.

He built me up with compliments and how much he missed me in the days leading up to the hotel visit. Because I was so naive, I was a "willing participant" to the "relationship" and advances. I was being groomed. In the state of Georgia, even as a "willing participant," I was not of age to consent to any relationship or sexual act being committed by either of them. At fourteen years old, I was too ignorant to understand how the law worked or what grooming was for that matter.

For reference, I was fourteen years of age, about 5'2 and was probably around 95 or 100 pounds. Even if I wanted to say no, I didn't stand a chance. At that point I wasn't saying no to Rob. I really thought this was normal. Why would I think otherwise? If Stan was allowed to do it, then what rules applied to others? I remember asking Rob one time why he was ok seeing me. His exact words: "You're mature for your age". A buzz phrase and total red flag for predators. Pedophiles don't think you're "mature". They like that you're naive and they use that to make underaged girls feel "grown-up" so they can entice you to do things they want.

But again, stranger danger didn't exist online or with people you know. That day in the hotel was the first time I realized Rob was capable of hurting me and not knowing when to stop. He had sex with me so many times and was so rough that he made me bleed and left me raw for days. Looking back on it now, I see just how degraded I really was.

He didn't have sex with me on the hotel room bed, because "the maids would have to remake the bed and they'd know I was in here." I was forced to have sex with him on the hotel floor, which not only produced carpet burns in the most uncomfortable places, but also taught me what my value to men at fourteen years old was.

In another instance, I met up with Rob again at a different extended stay hotel, where he was living. We hung out, he smoked what I thought was a joint but I'm not sure as I never touched it. He then grabbed me by the back of my head and hair, threw my face into his mattress, pulled down my pants and raped me anally. He pushed and held my face into the pillows and mattress to conceal my screams and cries. I don't remember how long this particular assault took place. I can only remember grabbing for the sheets, the bedding, anything I could to pull myself away from what was happening to me. I hurt physically for days after. Rob told me it was because it was my first time being penetrated anally. He apologized for being "too rough" and said it wouldn't happen again. I believed him, but I told him I didn't want to do that again. It hurt and I didn't like it.

While Rob never raped me anally again, that assault has stayed with me through adulthood. However, for the next eighteen months I continued to be groomed, manipulated, and used. Why did I continue to believe the man who had hurt me? The easy answer is he told me he loved me. The more complex answer is I wanted to be loved and I wanted to believe him. This was a man twice my age. I was fourteen and he was twenty-eight at the time this all started.

I saw kind words, good morning texts, and sweet gestures, so I accepted that you took the good with the bad. When I got sweet words, I thought of it as "romantic". I realize now I didn't know the meaning of the word. Books and movies had severely skewed what true love was for me, not counting the trauma of previous abuse. I did things with Rob sexually under the belief that I was "his world" and "he couldn't live without me." The harsh reality was he only wanted me because I was young and I continued to feed into the lie, so that he wouldn't go to prison.

I can't tell you the number of times Rob manipulated me into sex under the guise of "loving" me. I take my responsibility. I should have said no. I should have known better. I guess I didn't know how to stand up for myself and no one had certainly done anything to protect me. But again, in part, I do blame myself. I kept a lot close to my own chest and my own heart out of fear: fear of rejection, fear of not being believed, mainly for fear of wearing the tainted scarlet letter for life.

Maybe it's silly, but the #MeToo movement proved why so many girls don't speak up. We hide behind masks. We don't tear down our walls to let people in. Letting people in, believing all of the words, only set me up for more hurt and more distrust.

Rob and Stan were masters in the art of manipulation. Easily using the weaknesses of others to emotionally blackmail them. It didn't stop. It was like traveling in a maze, every turn led to a dead-end stop, and with each wrong stop, another form of abuse or blackmail was used. I couldn't win. I couldn't escape either of them. Imagine being thrown money for your birthday from a parent, but then having to "earn" that money with a sexual favor. Yes, Stan used me as a prostitute.

That year, I made a decision. I would move in with Stan. Sounds dumb right? It was. Moving in was clearly one of the worst decisions I could have made, but I was carrying a heavy mental burden. Because of that, I didn't want Stacy or my stepdad to question anything. My step dad, Greg, was a wonderful man, but at fourteen years old, I wanted to be a defiant butthead and "push back" in any way I could. My step dad made every attempt to be a dad to me, but for the longest time, I just would not have it. In part, because when he met Stacy, I wasn't trusting of anyone. It was around the same time that my sexual abuse started with Stan. I didn't let my guard down. He ended up being the safest person in my life. I just couldn't see that at fourteen though.

I had Rob, who I still trusted. And honestly due to the trauma, I just became an attitudinal, crappy teenager that didn't like being told what to do. So, I went to where I had both more freedom but was also a slave to the "master." I carried chains and while they may be metaphoric, they were real at the same time. Think back to the movie, A Christmas Carol, and you'll see the ghost of Jacob Marley adorned with chains and chests he has to carry with him. That was my existence in real life. And it's true what they say, you can never know what a person is really going through by social media or in pictures.

This was a time where Myspace was the big thing. I had a Myspace profile with my teenage dirtbag pictures. It's honestly hilarious now. I didn't fit anywhere. There weren't super in-tune or supportive parents, I didn't come from a rich family, but we weren't poor. I didn't have the nicest everything but had what I needed. I was neither overly smart, beautiful, tall, nor athletic. I was an outcast, the black sheep. I just didn't quite fit unless it involved a microphone.

Even then, that didn't apply with Stan. He didn't care if I had talent. He didn't care if I had potential. He just didn't care, period. I'm not sure If I was a disappointment being the only girl of all boys or if that's just who Stan was. I don't know if he's suffered his own trauma and just didn't break the cycle or if that's just who he is. I can't really say. I've never known him in a "dad" relationship, at least not the dad that taught me how to ride a bike, swing a bat, or walk me down the aisle on my wedding day. Maybe it's his own unresolved issues that carried over into adulthood. It's possible that his lack of empathy and harshness was nothing more than a taught survival tactic to protect himself. I have my theories, but they are nothing but just that….theories.

Chapter 6

The Move

That summer, I did, in fact, move in with Stan and his then girlfriend, who later became his wife. During the summer, they decided to buy a house. The house was a nice three-story in a housing complex with a quaint little walking path, a lake, and a park just across the street. When we moved in, I was offered the downstairs of the lowest story as it contained a bedroom, bathroom, another large room that could be a theater room and a smaller room, which later became a gym. I was the oldest of all the kids, so it made more sense for me to take that space. The middle floor was the main floor. It had the kitchen, living room, an office, a dining room, and a "poker" room. Stan wanted to go to the World Series of Poker, so he spent endless hours online playing. The top floor had a master bedroom, three smaller bedrooms, another bathroom, and the laundry room. My younger brothers stayed on the top floor with Stan and his pregnant girlfriend.

When we moved in, my room was this terrible Pepto-Bismol pink color. It would give one a headache just looking at it. Rob and I were still in touch but at some point, over the summer, he became angry at me for wanting to talk to him on the phone a lot. I was a teenager, what did he expect? He told me if he wanted to talk, he'd call me. I told him not to bother and I quit calling him altogether. The abuse from Stan didn't stop but I got away from Rob.

I started playing softball for a team, which I loved, but even in that, I was a loner. Stan only attended one game the whole season I played, and I was injured multiple times because he refused to provide me with all necessary equipment. On several occasions, I was knocked in the knees and shins because he wouldn't get me shin covers. Let me tell you, a softball going 90+ miles per hour careening into a knee-cap does not feel good.

Getting into the new house almost became worse for me. While I had softball and awesome friends, I was still abused, just in multiple different ways. I remember the time Stan was supposed to be hanging racks in my closet for my clothes. Stan's girlfriend took the little kids to the park. While she was gone, he raped me again, and again I counted cracks on the ceiling. As sick as it sounds, I prayed for the times he would bend me over and rape me so I wouldn't have to look him in the face. The disgust you feel for yourself is immeasurable when you're put into these situations. This is where I came to hate the dark, to hate locks, and to hate the sound of footsteps in the night. Because my room was on the bottom floor, I always locked my door. I always kept my closet or bathroom light on.

Stan worked nights in a club. Multiple nights a week he would come downstairs to my room to "check on things." I can't determine if it was my mind, my body, my ears, or my subconscious, but I became extremely hyper-aware of the sound of my lock clicking. So now, the sound of locks bothers me. Most people think of bothersome sounds, such as high pitched squeals or nails on a chalkboard, but the sounds of locks make my heartrate quicken, especially the push button locks that are loud, similar to the ones on restaurant bathrooms. In one instance, I tried to put something in front of my door to prevent him from coming in, forgetting about the bathroom door that granted access to my room. He was able to get right in.

While his pregnant girlfriend slept upstairs at two or three o'clock in the morning, I was awakened to be raped or to give oral favors. I didn't sleep much, and I started taking diet pills because Stan would "joke" or convince me I was fat. He bought them for me and told me to take them as instructed. The bottle instructed that I take up to fifteen pills per day.

Things that I never cared about before became important for Stan's acceptance. Stan would make comments about people having ugly feet. I started going to the nail salon with his girlfriend and having my toes done because I didn't want "gnarly" feet as he would call them. I will occasionally go get my nails done just to relax or for special occasions, but I am not, nor have I ever been, a glamor girl. I prefer jeans to dresses, boots to heels, and the clearance aisle to high-end clothing any day of the week. Makeup isn't something I care about.

Surprisingly, my grades were ok. I struggled in math, but Stan and girlfriend never bothered to help with homework or anything like that. His girlfriend wasn't exactly all that great to us either. We had more than our fair share of chores, including vacuuming all three stories every day because she had two dogs and a cat. She was "pregnant and couldn't do it." It was required that if they cooked, we cleaned the kitchen, did our own laundry and even theirs sometimes, as well as cleaning our rooms (which I never found unreasonable).

I do recall one time she helped me with a really neat project for school, but she wasn't motherly or loving in any way towards me or my brother closest to me in age. I had a conversation and asked Stan not to marry her, but instead, he went and told her what I said. I went to him as a daughter trying to have some semblance of real trust. She made damn sure to let me know she knew about my conversation with Stan. Not only did she confront me, but I caught much harder wrath and resentment from her after that. He did marry her.

So, now I had a step monster. Yes, I know that's harsh, but it is just to explain the way me and my brother were treated. They went and had family photos taken, leaving out only me and my brother closest in age to me. It was done with purpose because she made sure to show us the pictures as soon as they got them. Then, I became "the problem" when I said those weren't family pictures because the whole family wasn't there. The excuse was "you guys were at school" as if they couldn't schedule pictures in the evening or on a weekend. We were only included when it involved babysitting or cleaning. They also left me at fifteen years old at home with my twelve- or thirteen-year-old brother for about a week so they could take a family trip to her home state. Yes, Stan and my step monster left us alone for over a week. We had to walk to the store one day on a busy highway to get a few things from the store.

We knew how to fend for ourselves, but it wasn't the point. We were made to feel like a burden in our own home. Once my baby brother was born, it was a common occurrence to have her come down with a baby monitor and say "keep a listen out I'm going to the club to see your dad." An infant, a three-year-old, and a 12- or 13-year-old under my care at midnight or one AM, when I should have been sleeping for school. But if I wanted to go to the mall with friends, she got ugly about the curfew. Being an "adult" was fine until I wanted to do something with my friends and then I was "too young" to be out that late. The hypocritical double standard was omnipresent.

I meant it when I said I had not one nurturing person in my life at the time. The closest I ever remember getting to her was her helping me to do my makeup for a dance and helping me dye my hair. It wasn't her norm. I don't blame her now; in fact, I forgive her because just maybe I wasn't trusting enough to let her be nurturing. Not saying she would have been, but I had my guard up from the word go with her. It wasn't fair to her and in my growth as an adult, I can see now that I never really gave her a fair chance. It may have never made a difference but had I let her in just a little who knows, maybe it would have. It was second nature; most didn't stick around long, and Stan doesn't have the best marriage record. He's probably been married at least 10 or 15 times by now. I've never pulled the record although I probably could. I just don't care enough to know, because some things are not worth the chase or the investigation.

I've learned to read people like books, my reg flags go up immediately with certain people and maybe with her it did. I can't say. Maybe it was the mistreatment, maybe it was the lack of closeness, maybe I just didn't want to get close because closeness with anyone between either parent always led to disappointment and adjusting to a new person, home, or situation. It was never easy, and life felt so disposable at that time. It just was what it was.

Chapter 7

Could I Really Stay?

As the school year progressed, it became harder and harder to stay in that house. The almost nightly visits, the manipulation, the scare tactics. There was a basic knowledge that no one in that house cared about me or my brother for any other reason than to be a maid or a hole for their taking. I cried a lot, I also blamed myself because I was too scared to speak up and too terrified of what would happen.

I became a shell of myself completely closed off to most everyone around me. I dyed my hair black and wore black clothing almost all the time. It wasn't a phase or trying to fit into a clique; it was exactly how I felt, empty and dark. I chose to put myself in that environment and I take full responsibility for thinking that things would get better if I showed that I was in some way worthy. I guess deep down I thought if Stan saw that I wasn't a bad "kid," he would realize his mistakes in using me like trash or he would just get tired of me altogether but neither ever happened.

I was accepted into a great performing arts school. I had a new opportunity to study music and continue to do what I really loved. Attending the school meant staying in that house of horror. My other option was to move back in with Stacy, where at least I wasn't being abused physically everyday.

When I had finally weighed the options enough, I concluded that I had to leave the hell in which I lived. This wasn't an easy decision for me. I had to audition for the performing arts school and had been accepted. I remember opening the acceptance letter and no one in Stan's house was happy or excited for me. Support in every form was lacking from that home. There were no celebrations for bringing home championship wins for my softball team nor getting into the performing arts school. I'm not that person who "needs a cookie" for every accomplishment in life, but while the younger kids and baby were doted on and encouraged, it seemed as though we older kids were just forgotten. We were the lepers of the family if you'd even call it a family.

I just could not tolerate being an inconvenience in the home until I was convenient. Take softball as a good example. Stan dropped me off on a Saturday morning for a game, he didn't stay and attend like most parents did. When the game was over, I called him to come pick me up. I was told to find my own way home. Thankfully I had a teammate that could drive, and she agreed to take me home, otherwise I would have been left on the ball field with no way to get home. While I understand that abuse comes in far worse forms than not having a ride home, it was absolutely still abuse. As a parent now my kids barely leave my sight beyond school or the occasional babysitter, so I can't fathom leaving my child at a ball field to fend for themselves. Uber and Lyft didn't exist when I was fifteen years old.

The decision was made but under one condition. I had to wait until the end of the school year. So I did. At that time I had a boyfriend who took me to his homecoming. He was in high school, and I was in middle school. He was also terrible to me but it wasn't any worse than the way I was treated any other day. Rob popped back up saying "he missed me." He was sick because "he couldn't live without me". I used it to my advantage. Why not? I let him take me to the mall and buy my homecoming dress.

I'll villainize myself here for a moment. I was a self-centered and selfish teenager with a bitterness towards most people. I had been used and taught how to use people. I played the game. I take back what I said earlier, Stan did teach me one thing, he taught me the art of not caring and manipulation, basically, how to get my way.

Stacy was no better in that teaching. She would use men to her own advantage until they didn't fit the bill anymore. It's not something I'm proud of today. It's not someone I am or that I desire to be. I killed that manipulative, self-centered, person years ago. Not physically of course, but I killed that terrible person mentally and psychologically. Due to my upbringing with a lack of empathy and just overall caring, I became the very person I hated so much in my bio parents. I had a real "I don't give a shit" attitude. I didn't care if I used people for my own gain and I didn't care if it hurt other people. I took money from Stan feeling like he owed me after using me. I allowed Rob to spend money on me not caring if he was around or not. The world had dealt the shitty hand and if I could improve it with money, gifts, or things I wanted, I was going to take it and allow them to pay for it. I was an awful person, but it was without a doubt anger towards those who hurt me and the feeling of being "owed."

No one, and I mean NO one, owed or owes me anything and it took me a long time to figure that out. I used my abusers to my advantage. Some of it was survival mode, some of it was utter defeat, and some was just acceptance that this was how things were. It was going to happen anyway so why not gain something from it? Again, I was a wretched human. I'll always own that, and I'll never be proud of it. It took me years into my adulthood to realize that by accepting "help" from my abusers that I was really just living under their control just like when I was a teenager. Even in my adult years, I've asked both bio parents for help and it was useless. The help they gave was financial, but it was met with eyerolls and holding it over my head. I guess neither got the memo that it isn't "help" if you use it to hold it over someone for years. I take nothing from either of them anymore, I don't want to. I'm done being controlled by what they can give me financially. They can give money. Not love, support, and definitely not acknowledgement of anything either of them did wrong.

The decision was made, yes I would move back in with Stacy and my step dad. Even that home situation wasn't ideal. Neither of them knew about the sexual abuse or the trauma I carried, which I never blamed them for, but Stacy was extremely critical about everything and still is to this day. Her abuse wasn't in the form of sexual abuse, it was more verbal than anything. While dealing with sexual and physical abuse, verbal abuse can be just as bad. It beats you down to nothing. Physical abuse hurts, but that physical pain eventually goes away. Verbal and psychological abuse stay in your mind for years, if not forever.

At some point, I don't remember the timeline, but Rob convinced me he missed me so much and couldn't live without me and we reconnected. He had to leave the state for a while due to his financial situation, but when I moved back in with Stacy over the summer, he followed and got a place just a few miles away from my house. Rob didn't have a car or a license for that matter. I had a learner's permit so some days during the summer I would take the truck from Stacy's home and go meet him and hang out with him. It was wrong, stupid, and completely unlawful, but grooming will cause an otherwise intelligent and responsible teenager to do stupid things. I was convinced that Rob loved me. Another lie by another predator.

I spent most of that summer alone or with Rob. It was slightly more tolerable than where I was. Rob had convinced me that as soon as I turned 18, we would get married. He even went as far as giving me a ring. I had spoken to his mother on the phone. To my knowledge, his family knew he "loved" someone but had no clue about my age. That was all kept a lie. Of course, I played along. I knew revealing myself would ultimately lead to charges and imprisonment for Rob. So again, I kept quiet.

I walked through life being invisibly bound by ropes, chains, and duct tape. I didn't know what love was. I knew what attention was. This is the twisted existence that pedophiles use to capture prey. The more vulnerable, damaged, and attention-seeking a young person is, the easier it is to fully take control of them. I knew that the attention I was getting from Rob was better than what Stan was giving me. Or at least that's what I thought. I thought I knew what love looked like with Rob. It was just more manipulation, more mind games and more mistreatment that I thought was love. Everything about the situation was a lie. I honestly thought someone cared, I thought someone loved me. Looking back at it now, I was a stupid, young, naive little girl who didn't understand the world or its dangers. The majority of my summer was spent stealing Stacy and my step dad's truck and meeting up with Rob. We smoked pot, had sex, and hung out. I had it in my mind that I knew it all. Like most teenagers, I thought I knew best. I thought I was invincible and nothing could go wrong. Nothing bad could happen to me. I didn't understand the repercussions of my actions. Point blank - not only was I an idiot, but I was an idiot committing crimes. Another thing I'm not proud of.

Summer came and went. It was almost time to start back school. Stan drove down to help go school shopping. That didn't come without a price either. I was raped in Stacy's house in order to get school clothes and school supplies. I regretted instantly that I asked him to take me shopping. At this point I did have a learner's permit so after the rape in my own home I had to drive us both to go school shopping. He slept the whole way there and then handed me money to go get what I wanted and needed so he could sleep more. Once we got back to my house, I was then forced to perform oral favors for the money he spent on my clothes. Frankly, I was no better than a hooker at this point. Stan provided no extras without "favors." Apparently spending money on school clothes was an extra not a necessity so "favors" were required. He didn't like the things Stacy bought me, he said they look cheap but his money didn't provide for free.

I became even more distant in my own home, where I should have been most comfortable. I closed myself off in my room. It was far easier to escape into nothingness with just me, my music, and my phone, where I talked to my friends and Rob. Stacy worked a lot and so did my stepdad (I don't fault either of them for that) but I was alone a lot and that gave me more opportunities to make poor choices and find trouble. That's exactly what I did getting mixed up with Rob. Even if Stacy and my step dad didn't see it, I was headed down a slippery slope and fast. I was setting myself up for failure and that's exactly what was about to happen.

Chapter 8

High School

In the fall of 2006, I started the 9th grade.
There were tons of people I knew in my high
school because I went to school with them in
middle school before my move. Majority of them
were a year ahead of me at this point because I
repeated 8th grade. I really struggled in school once
my sexual abuse started. It was difficult to focus on
schoolwork when you know the things that have
happened to you at home.

High school was short lived for me too.
School started in August and by the end of August
or early September, I was listed as an endangered
runaway. I know that sounds like some sort of
"rebel without a cause" or some juvenile delinquent
with no proper upbringing. Despite the fact that I
didn't really have much of an upbringing, I was far
from a delinquent. I had never been in trouble with
the law, I was an honor chorus student, and had
never been in any real trouble from any of my

family. Sure, there was the occasional lecture of how to be an upstanding citizen. Don't lie, cheat, or steal, but to me, those were just words when you had parents that managed to do all of the above. It was a do as I say, not as I do lecture.

To deal with the trauma of my abuse, I turned to smoking pot. Another one of those things I'm not really proud of, but it's my truth and I said I would be raw and real about my story. My stepdad had his suspicions of me smoking pot and questioned me on it. I admitted I was smoking, and he wanted a name of who I was getting it from. He truly cared, I just didn't see that. I couldn't give him a name because that name was Rob. By naming Rob, the house of cards would start to fall. So, I gave him the bogus name of Josh claiming I didn't know Josh's last name. Josh was a common enough name, so it was easy to just name it. My stepdad gave me until the end of the next school day to produce Josh's last name or he would go to the school himself. I knew I was just digging my hole deeper, but I was panicking and couldn't admit to what was really happening to me. Admission made everything real. It meant I couldn't be invisible anymore; I couldn't pretend things were ok, I couldn't just sit in my room and drown myself in music in attempts to rid myself of hellish memories. It also meant by revealing Rob, I'd be revealing the things Stan had done to me too. I was more scared of him. Rob could easily run and never be heard from again, but Stan would ultimately call me a liar and I would be accused of mistruths. THIS was my biggest fear after all the threats and manipulations.

I was told I would lose my entire family. I would never see Stacy or my brothers again. Stan never specified what that meant. Was he threatening to kill me? Or threatening to harm those I loved? I still, to this day, 16 years later, have no clue how to answer that question. All I knew was that these manipulation tactics scared me more than the abuse. That's a sad existence. I don't even know if you'd call that an existence. There were times I just wanted to be dead. Not that I wanted to hurt myself, I've never had to desire to hurt myself, but I just didn't want to exist anymore.

Too many teen girls today live with these thoughts after abuse. My goal in this book isn't to baffle, hurt, trigger or harm anyone but to make those who have experienced similar trauma realize that the journey isn't always easy, but it is possible. With that being said, this story is about to get harder before it gets easier.

Chapter 9

Endangered Runaway

I was an anxious teen. I wasn't a
rule-breaker and I wasn't a bad person, or at least I
didn't think so at the time, but I was truly making
bad decisions at this point and time. In part, I can
blame it on trauma and the need to hide myself
from the world. Most importantly, I hid from those
in my family. I thought they would judge me and
not with a fair scope. I honestly believed that Stacy
and my stepdad would not believe what had
happened to me. After being told I had by the end
of the school day to produce a name, I got scared
and called Rob from my friend's cell phone at
school. He said he was on his way to get me. But he
had no car, so he had to walk, and I needed a place
to hide.

I asked another friend if I could sit in his
van until someone arrived with pads for me, telling
him that I had just started my period. This was a
complete lie, but he agreed and asked me to lock

the doors to the van when I was done. I sat there and waited until I spotted Rob. Once I spotted him, I had to carefully sneak through the surplus of cars in the school parking lot. I snuck through them with ease, which wasn't hard due to my small stature. Lifted trucks were a big deal at my high school. The only thing I had to worry about was not getting caught by the school resource officer, which I had gotten caught by before leaving school on my own because I felt sick one day and was attempting to walk home.

I held my breath as I slowly snuck through the cars, across the small plain of grass, and across the asphalt. Once with Rob, we immediately got out of the view of the school. From there, we had to make a plan. Rob successfully snuck me into his house, which was one big house with multiple tenants renting rooms and sharing communal areas such as the kitchen. Rob left me in the room and walked to my house and grabbed the clothes I would need. We also dyed my hair black to alter my appearance. People would be looking for a red head not a girl with black hair. I never made it home that night. I stayed with Rob preparing to run away. I was reported missing as an endangered runaway.

The next morning, the police showed up at Rob's place. How could I have been found so quickly? I hid in another person's room. I wasn't found by the police. I slowly snuck up to the door to see the police, Stacy, my stepdad, and Rob talking to each other on the porch of the giant home. I crept with such ease, they never saw or heard me, mere feet away from them. Rob, of course, lied about knowing me and claiming he hadn't seen me. Rob fabricated some story about "Josh" bringing me to his residence once. After the police left, Rob instructed me to go out the back door, slide through the broken wooden fence, cross the street, and walk up the abandoned railroad tracks until I found the bridge and to hide under it. I did as instructed.

Once I made it to the railroad tracks and found the bridge, I climbed under the bridge and waited for what seemed like forever until I saw Rob. I suppose he took a different route or stayed behind a little longer, just in case the police were watching him. Rob wasn't due to receive a paycheck for two more days, so for two days I slept under a bridge in the dirt. When we finally emerged after two days, I was disgusting, covered in red Georgia clay from my head to my feet. Rob grabbed his paycheck and bought us something to eat. From there he got us a cab and had it take us to a greyhound station where we boarded a bus headed for Indiana.

I was dirty, tired but thankful for a comfortable bus seat to lay in and the opportunity to get some sleep. I don't remember much about the ride on the Greyhound, except for the millions of trees that dotted the rolling hills of Kentucky. I also recall that my first meal once arriving in Indianapolis was White Castle, which I had never had before. Rob told me we were going to a friend's house in another part of Indiana. That was the first time in three days that I was able to shower and get all that red dirt off of me and I was able to really sleep.

Chapter 10

Endangered Run-Away to Kidnapped

After three days of running from some of my demons, I told Rob maybe I needed to go home and accept everything, tell Stacy and my stepdad what happened, and why I ran. I just needed to spill my guts. I was exhausted physically, mentally, and emotionally. Rob told me I couldn't go back home and that he would go to prison. I believe he told me this because he still didn't know about what Stan had done to me. I believe he thought I wanted to go home to reveal him, but either way I was told no.

I don't know how Rob's friends found out I was a "runaway" or that I was only fifteen years old, but the female whose name I don't recall all these years later, confronted me and pushed me to the ground. This confirmed my worst fear....the child would be blamed, not the grown man. I ran away from their apartment and Rob chased after telling me "it would all be ok, and he would protect me." I asked him again if he could get me home and his response was the same: that he'd go to prison.

I can't remember how many days I walked. We walked for what seemed like forever. I was dirty, starving, and my knee that had been injured years before in a rollerblading accident was starting to swell. I told Rob I couldn't walk anymore. This was the moment I realized Rob was far more sinister than I realized. His idea was to strike, gag, and bind an elderly person and rob them for money, their car, and anything else he could get from them. I didn't like this idea. While I wasn't a very empathic teen, I didn't have it in my heart to harm anyone and I told him that wasn't a clever idea. He suggested using duct tape and making a small hole where he could place a straw so "hopefully they didn't die" these were his exact words.

This wasn't the Rob I knew, and I had never heard him speak of such sinister or malice acts before. This was the true danger I had put myself in. That is the danger of chat rooms and pedophiles. I was in complete shock and protested hurting anyone. That was not who I was and it's not who I am today.

Due to my adamance about not physically harming anyone, I was made to walk more. I don't know how many miles were covered in a day, but it felt like a ton. We dipped into dollar stores or retail stores, and I did more that I'm not proud of. I stole things like clean underwear, clean clothes, and little bits of food like crackers and chicken salad packs just so I could eat. I was in survival mode again. I was doing things that were against every part of myself morally.

When you're put in those situations, you do things to survive, things that you aren't proud to do. When faced with the choice of stealing crackers or watching Rob harm someone, I chose stealing crackers. During the miles of walking, I was told to look for a certain type of root. I don't recall the name of it now but apparently it was worth money. If I complained about the pain in my knee, I was dragged aggressively by my arm and told to keep going.

I was a southern girl, born and raised, trapped in a northern state and the weather was harsh on me. It was only September, but the air was far colder than it would have been in Georgia. All attempts to keep me going were failing. I was sleeping on cardboard boxes behind department stores. Rob did attempt to bend them in a way that would form a makeshift tent to radiate heat, but it was useless. My body was not built for a fall or winter in the north.

The next day it was back to walking, which meant more miles. As the day progressed, my knee was swelling worse and to top it off, I was starting to get sick. At nightfall, I got to rest behind the dumpster of a Hardee's. Sleeping behind a dumpster is an ultimate low but I found solace in it because it meant rest. It meant I could rest my knee and try to get warm from the cold. When you're so tired and your body is so physically exhausted, sleeping behind a dumpster doesn't seem like a big deal. You ignore the stench of trash and leftover food, and you just sit. I hated this situation, but I blamed myself. I had come to recognize just how capable Rob was of hurting someone so when he laid on top of me "to keep me warm." It felt more like a way to keep me from running. I slept behind a dumpster, on a box, in the rain, with an almost 200-pound man on top of me.

The following morning, the sun was shining, and I was thankful for what little warmth it provided. My knee and my cold were worse than they had been up to this point. Rob made the decision that he was going to steal a car. So, he waited, and he watched as patrons entered and exited the Hardee's after picking up their morning breakfast. After some time watching, he observed a man exit an older white Chevy Cavalier - the man had left the keys in it. I didn't like the idea of stealing a car, but no one would get hurt this way and my body just physically could not walk any more. When the middle-aged, dark-haired man turned his back to the car to fill up his drink at the soda dispenser, we both made a run for it and Rob stole a car.

I know it was wrong, I know it should have never happened, but I was so thankful for the heat, for the ability to rest my knee, and thankful for not being forced to walk miles a day. I knew karma would catch up with us. It was just a matter of time. People who do terrible things receive terrible things. What you put into this world will pay you back. Karma owed me big time. Maybe that's why I was in the situation I was in. I was a dreadful person, and I was deserving of what I was receiving.

Inside the car, Rob found a checkbook, instructed me to write him checks, and sign them under the check holder's name. Like I said, karma owed me. I'm 100% absolutely ashamed of this act but my objection was met with anger, and I was scared of the repercussions. He had just suggested hitting an elderly person with a rock so he could rob them and "hopefully they didn't die." I was petrified. On top of being in survival mode, I still believed that I loved Rob. I'll never be able to explain that. Predators know exactly how to

manipulate young girls into infatuation. I wrote
and signed the checks.

I suppose he was pretty proud of himself.
He kept saying, "I told you I'd provide for you."
Yeah, I was really living the dream: sleeping behind
dumpsters and now riding in a stolen car. After
cashing the few checks he had me write, his biggest
concern was getting out of Indiana. I went to sleep.
I was so tired. There is really no way to describe
how exhausted I was or how much pain I was in.
It's indescribable. All I remember directly after
stealing that car was wanting to get warm,
wanting to sleep and waiting for the moment when
law enforcement would finally catch up with us.
When they did, we'd deserve everything that was
coming to us. But for now, I was warm and I could
sleep on something other than a dumpster or
cardboard box. I had no clue where we were headed
but I knew we were literally riding on borrowed
time.

Chapter 11

Journey Across the Country

When I finally woke up, the first place we were was Chicago. I had never seen anything but my home state of Georgia, Florida, and Tennessee. My knowledge of the northern states was minimal. Once in Chicago, Rob wanted to take me to see the Pier. We found a place to park the stolen ride and walked to the pier and then down to the sand. As we did, the sky turned to a dark, angry, threatening gray. The thunder was so loud it was deafening. A storm was coming. After minutes of being on the Chicago pier, we were sprinting back to the car soaked from the sudden deluge of rain. We drove around Chicago for a few hours just seeing the buildings and the sights of Chicago. It's the only time I've ever been, even though I hated the circumstances. I vaguely remember entering New York state, but not into New York City. For reasons unknown, he decided to change course and head back west. He said for Seattle. What I know now is that Seattle is a city for lost kids. Lots of runaways or dumped kids reside there. I'm not sure if that was his plan but it seems like the most likely scenario now.

I can't remember the collective order of which states, cities, or towns we entered so bear with me on these memories. In all I believe I entered into 19 states total. Some we just drove through and some we stayed awhile. I can't remember which state it was. It may have been Iowa or Wisconsin, but it was filled with beautiful prairie-type lands with beautiful landscapes and small towns. We'd enter one town and the sign would read, "Population: 112." Those towns were fascinating to me. Everyone went to the same school, they would have one gas station, and there would be kids as young as 13 or 14 driving tractors to till the land. It was a completely unique way of life from mine. So simplistic, yet so beautiful. At certain points along the way, Rob would pull off to secluded areas to rape me or force me to get on top of him.

I can't remember the town or even the state for that matter, but this little place was having some sort of town festival with a parade, food, and all kinds of stuff. He stopped and wanted to check things out. While we were walking around, a lady was giving away a dog and a cat. Rob took them both for me saying he thought they would do me well and give me company. I guess he could sense I wanted to be home. I missed home.

Now don't get me wrong, I got to see some beautiful places and people on this journey, but I missed home. I refer to this time as a journey because it took me to places and sights I'll never forget…even the bad stuff. I now had a cat and a dog. While they did give me company and I loved them, we could barely feed ourselves, much less two animals. I don't know how he thought that would work, but he got them. Small towns like these were easy to feed ourselves. Walking into a store and grabbing mayo, bologna and bread was easy without being seen.

Again, I don't remember the exact state, but we had stopped at a QuikTrip to use the bathroom. As I was getting out of the car, the cat had gotten between the seat and the door. When I went to close the door, I accidentally closed the door on the cat. Now anyone who knows me knows I'm a huge animal lover and would never harm an animal on purpose. Rob instantly freaked out on me claiming, "you tried to kill my cat". He not only beat me for this incident, but he also drove me to the nearest vet and tried to make me leave it outside their office. They were closed. When I got out to leave the cat there for help, Rob tried to leave me in the middle of nowhere. A place I didn't know and no way to go. I was scared and begged him not to leave me or that poor cat. He let both me and the cat back in the car. He found a secluded area and hit me multiple times for being "cruel to his cat". It was completely accidental but somehow it was still my fault. Thankfully the cat made a full recovery, and she was fine. I wish I could say the same for myself.

Rob managed to steal a tent from a Walmart, so we spent a lot of time camping. This made it easier for him to seclude me from the public. He often took us to KOAs ("Kampgrounds of America") to stay so we could shower. This one was hard for me. I was not allowed to shower alone. I had a 6-foot 5-inch tall man standing over me watching as I cleaned myself. And I didn't get to clean myself often: once a week if I was lucky.

I will absolutely admit I've done many things I'm not proud of. I've stolen clothes to have clean ones, I've done dine and dash to eat. The shame I feel for those things are immense even today. Survival mode will make you do things to ensure you survive, especially when you aren't sure if someone is capable of harm. Rob, just days before, spoke of harming an elderly person, so who knew what he was truly capable of? And while I wanted to go home, I also embraced the people I met and the things I got to see. I thought this was my new life, I didn't fight back, I didn't argue. Small incidences would set Rob off and I did not want to test what he was fully capable of.

South Dakota was a beautiful place where I got to see Mt. Rushmore and the Crazy Horse monument. It's a very odd fight with yourself to be both homesick and manipulated by someone you think you love. You deal with the abuse both physical and sexual because you think they care. It took me years to recognize that someone that loves and cares for you does not do those things. Rob did NOT love me; he did NOT care about me. He had groomed, manipulated, and coerced me into believing that he would protect and love me forever, but he beat me over an accident. That's not love. But at this point I didn't feel like I could get away. By the middle of September, I had been through about 19 states across the U.S. twice. You read that correctly we had driven through each one twice. This trip was coming to an end and we didn't even know it.

Chapter 12

The Final Destination

In mid-September, we stopped at a place in Montana ironically called Lake Ashley. It was a camping spot, so we set up the tent, made a fire, and enjoyed the scenery. I will say this, you can't look at a place like Lake Ashley or the mountains of Montana and not believe in God or a higher power. The waters of lake Ashley were crystal clear and had a beautiful, emerald green hue. It was the most beautiful thing I have ever seen. This was the place that gave me hope. I had been missing from my home for almost six weeks. In this place though I felt a peace like I had not in over two years. For two years, I had dealt with abuse and trauma but somehow this place in a moment made those things feel insignificant like I could defeat those things. I swear that place had healing waters. Maybe not for the physical, but definitely for the soul.

While at Lake Ashley, I met a man. He was Native American and one of the nicest men I had ever met. I wish I could remember his name. I don't know if he sensed something wrong with me or my soul. I don't know if he could tell I was abused, or just felt something within himself. With a feather, Indian leather, and paint, he sat and recreated the lake we overlooked on that feather in paint. When he finished, he gave it to me. He told me it would always protect me. I truly have a love for the Native American community and the love they show. He knew nothing of me. He had no idea I was damaged; I was trash, I was abused, raped, and I was a bad person. All he saw was the need to give me something that would protect me. I slept that night beneath the stars, with crickets singing, against the crackle of the fire beside the most beautiful lake and mountains I have ever seen. Somehow, I knew everything would be ok.

Lake Ashley was the final stop before the end of this journey. Rob took us into Billings, Montana, where we stopped at an Olive Garden to dine and dash. We ate, not knowing it would be the last night we would ever see each other. We ate, not knowing I would wake up and start to understand that this 30-year-old man was not a man who loved me but a man who wanted to take everything from me, including my childhood. Because we literally had no money, dine and dash and stealing gas was the norm. Rob would also pick through the ashtrays that were left outside restaurants for cigarettes because he was a smoker. Before our dine and dash at Olive Garden Rob picked through the ashtray for an after-dinner cigarette. He grabbed a few and put them into an empty pack he had found. We ate and ran out when it was busy, and people weren't paying attention. We got "good" at knowing the busy times, so it was easy to leave unnoticed.

As we left the parking lot at a rapid pace, I had no clue where we were headed. The next destination had not been decided. Rob jumped on the interstate to get away from our dine and dash location as quickly as possible. As he got on the interstate, he lit that after dinner cigarette and smoked it. As he finished it, he threw it out the window like most smokers do. This was the catalyst that would end six weeks of fear, abuse, and in a weird way, peace. I know some will never understand the peace part, but I saw places that literally gave my soul peace. It wasn't the person I was with, it wasn't the rapes, the beatings, or the mistreatment. It was the beauty I had seen in both places and people. It was God showing himself through those places and people.

That lit cigarette thrown out the window was my rescue. As it would happen, a police officer saw Rob throw the lit cigarette out the window and that was his pet peeve. The land in Montana is so dry that a lit cigarette can cause wildfires and that miniscule act of tossing it from the car is illegal. Suddenly, blue lights were behind us. I panicked.

While this was my rescue away from the man who was hurting me, it was also the man who I thought was going to protect me and take me away from all bad happening to me at home. I was so scared I told him to drive and begged him not to let "them" get me. He didn't understand that sentence. He thought "them" was the police, but "them" was Stan and my family because I feared so badly not being believed, I feared what awaited me back in Georgia. I missed home terribly, but fear gripped me like a hostage. I had so many fears at that moment that I begged a man who had treated me so badly and had preyed on me to save me. In no way will a predator or abuser ever be your savior. There is only one Savior and he was about to show out in my life big time.

Chapter 13

Modern-day Bonnie and Clyde

When I said don't let them get me, Rob punched it and the chase was on. What started as one police car quickly became two, then five, and the numbers kept stacking against the one car we were in. He made every attempt to lose them. Multiple times, patrol cars attempted to PIT us (Precision Immobilization Technique - where a police officer uses their vehicle to spin out the fleeing vehicle). Rob somehow managed to avoid those PIT attempts. The number of patrol cars behind us were growing by the minute. It was nothing but blue, strobing lights as far as the eye could see. A Fourth of July fireworks show had competition with the lights that illuminated the highway that September night. He said he would pull over and told me to run towards them screaming for help. I told him no; they would send me back home with Stan. The look on his face was so confused. It was at that moment I told him I wanted to run because Stan had been raping me for the last two years and was knowledgeable of my relationship with Rob. I was blackmailed. If I didn't continue to do sexual favors for Stan, he would turn Rob into law enforcement. Ultimately, I was being controlled by two vicious men who didn't have a care in the world for me.

This chase lasted a total of 67 miles and included 22 patrol cars before spike strips were deployed to bring the car safely to a stop. God protected me that night. Had a PIT maneuver been successful, I may not be here today to tell my story. When I exited the vehicle with my hands up, I had 22 guns pointed in my face. When asked who I was, I said a runaway from Georgia and acted as if I didn't care that I adorned silver bracelets. I was still so manipulated. I was trying to protect my kidnapper. As I was placed in handcuffs and the officer walked me to his patrol car, he escorted me past the patrol car Rob was in. We both mouthed that we loved each other. This scene in my head now makes me angry and disappointed in the sixteen year old me. I really thought I loved this person. I wasn't worried about myself. I could have been killed, but in that moment, death seemed insignificant compared to facing my biggest monster which was Stan. I couldn't see in those moments that Rob and Stan were the same person. They were both monsters stealing the innocence of young girls.

I was taken to a detention center where I was booked in as a juvenile. I was never offered any sort of medical attention, I was just booked in. They were able to call Stacy and I was allowed to talk to her for about five minutes. I told her about Stan over the phone and at first, she didn't believe me. Not that I was surprised, it was the reaction I feared and expected. She then accused me of being high on drugs. Something I didn't do. Yes, I have admittedly said I've smoked pot before, but at that time I was clean as a whistle and was furious. I wanted someone to listen, so I lashed out. I raised my voice and I yelled. I was mad at the situation. I was mad at myself. I was mad that no one was listening. I was also mad that someone I believed I loved was also a monster in my story. Which I had not accepted yet. That acceptance didn't come until later, after quite some time in counseling.

I was a scared, and frankly pissed, 15-year-old girl. I had never been in trouble before this. I was sitting in a jail cell. That was the karma catching up to me for all the terrible things I had done. I was crushed, but I also felt worthy of the punishments I received. Even though I was scared of the things I would have to talk about, I had to play hard. I was in jail with real criminals. Some of these teens were there for attempted murder. In group time, I put on this front like I was a badass, and proudly announced I was a runaway from Georgia that had just gotten arrested for being in a 67-mile police chase. Insert facepalm here. I WAS DUMB!!!!! I was acting like I was a true hard ass, when in all reality I was a scared little girl, I was scared of everything at this point. I was scared of my own life and what was about to become of it.

******Below is an article written by the Billings Gazette about the night of the police chase. I wanted to add this to further validate my story. Billings Gazette gave me permission to use the article and I've blacked out the true identity of my kidnapper to ensure his privacy.********

MHP catches suspect after pursuit

Gazette News Services Sep 22, 2006

The Montana Highway Patrol arrested an Indiana man Thursday night after a high-speed chase on Interstate 90 that started near Laurel and ended near Big Timber, when the vehicle drove over spike strips.

No one was injured during the 67-mile pursuit. Officers arrested the driver, █████████████, of Universal, Ind., who was driving a Chevrolet Cavalier reported stolen from Indiana. ██████ also had outstanding warrants from Georgia, a patrol spokesman said Friday. ▮ was booked into the Yellowstone County jail.

A 15-year-old girl also was taken into custody. She was with ▮ voluntarily, the patrol said.

The chase started at 8:14 p.m. near Laurel after a traffic offense, the patrol said. Average speeds were between 85 and 95 mph and topped 100 mph. The chase slowed briefly as it went through Laurel, the patrol said.

Joining the patrol in the pursuit were Laurel and Columbus police officers and the sheriff's deputies from Stillwater and Sweet Grass counties.

The chase ended after ▮ vehicle drove over spike strips put out by the Sweet Grass County Sheriff's Department. The vehicle rolled to a stop as the tires flattened. Officers arrested ▮ without further incident, the patrol said.

Chapter 14

The FBI and the man that cried

While in lockup, I was visited by two FBI agents for an interview. I don't remember their names or much about their appearances at all. Those days were a blur. Locked in a cinderblock cage, for 23 hours a day, with nothing more than a metal toilet and a large slab of cinder block that held a gym mat for sleeping. I spent most of my time reading. The Bible mostly. I hadn't really been brought up in church or been taught much about God but the remorse for my actions ate at me so viciously that I had to search for the forgiveness and the answers I desired. I didn't know of God's love or promises for me, but it was becoming clearer with every passing verse and book in the Bible.

The two men that visited me from the FBI were full of questions about my relationship with Rob, our travels, and the things that happened.

They seemed most intrigued by what I was telling them involving Stan. Maybe that was of more interest to them because it made the puzzle make sense or maybe because it was a new case for them to pursue. They listened as much as I wanted to talk and allowed me the room to fill in as much detail as I could in my own words. They did as any good detective does, they listened. Both were nice, clearly having a good set of skills to perform the jobs they did. They informed me that they had interviewed Rob. He would tell them everything, I was sure of it. He would tell them just "how much he loved me". I believed they were just confirming his story. I questioned them on what he had told them, and they informed me nothing. Absolutely zero. I believe, in fact, he "lawyered up" right away and refused to talk to them. I couldn't believe it. Here I was defending "us" with everything I had, and he wouldn't say one word. I believe I even tried to defend our age difference by proclaiming that people like Jerry Lee Lewis had married his 13-year-old cousin. Good gravy, what was I thinking? Blinded by ignorance, I swore it was the hill I'd die on.

One evening as I was sitting in my cell reading and praying, my cell door opened. One of the guards had come to get me and informed me of a visitor. Who in the world would be visiting me so late? It was later than the normal visiting hours for the detention center. It was one of the FBI agents who had visited me earlier. I wasn't expecting him and he was without his partner, which struck me as odd but I was happy to be out of my cell, even if it was just for a short period of time. I wish like crazy I could remember that FBI agent's name. He's the first person I recall actually caring. I was expecting another barrage of questions involving the case against Rob. Instead, this grown man sat across from me and just wept. He was crying for me. He told me he was a father to a daughter who was the same age as me and he couldn't imagine her going through what I had. It was the reason he got up everyday and did his job.

This man has stuck with me for years. Not in appearance or name, but in his caring for someone beyond himself. Detectives, agents, and officers often carry one case with them for life. The one case that keeps them awake at night and I'm not sure if my case was his, but I'd be willing to guess it's probable, purely based on the emotions that man radiated. It was against everything they taught him. They are taught to do the job and to be almost robotic in response. They are human. Those human emotions save more people than most people realize. They often don't get the credit they deserve for it either. This particular man didn't have a hand in "saving" me but what he taught me may have been far more important: there is more good than bad in the world and people do care. I wish I could remember his name or had a way to get in touch with him to thank him, but I don't. I can only hope that for the good he put out in this world, he received it back many times over and that he's been blessed beyond belief.

My stay in Montana was short-lived. I was there for about two weeks for interviews and statements. I was a minor and forced into criminal acts such as writing checks so I was treated as a victim in my case. I still carried guilt. While I understand the coercion now, I still carry guilt for the bad I have done. The car chase took place on September 22nd, 2006, and on October 1st, I was being flown home. The FBI flew Stacy to Montana to meet me and for the first time in six weeks, I felt somewhat safe. From Montana, we had a connecting flight to Colorado, and then back to my home state of Georgia. Finally, after six weeks of running from fear, running from the demons, running from everything bad that had ever happened to me, I was home. It was time to face the demons that haunted me. I was back to something familiar. I still had a lot more ahead of me, but this was a start.

It was a start to some healing for me. I guess first was acceptance. I had to accept that Rob didn't love me, he groomed me and used me. I had to accept that I didn't love him, I only loved what I thought was a good relationship. I had to accept my faults, my mess-ups, my issues, and, worst of all, every demon that haunted me. Demons to most are fictional storybook characters or scary images in movies. Mine were real. They visited my thoughts and tortured me in dreams. Sleep isn't your friend when you live a life stalked by demons because they visit occasionally and take you back to places you don't want to revisit. The things that happened are seared into the brain cells as if branding cattle on a ranch. The marks are there forever, even if they lie below the surface completely unseen by anyone else. They still exist. No amount of time erases it. It just becomes somewhat more tolerable as the years pass for some. For others, it tortures them into far more hurtful acts like drugs or suicide. Some just can't live with that kind of torture.

Chapter 15

The Not-So-Sweet 16

I returned home on my 16th birthday. It was entirely uneventful, yet exactly what I needed. I remember Stacy asking what I wanted for my birthday. My answer was a hot shower, chicken and dumplings, a homemade chocolate cake, and a bed. That is exactly how I spent my 16th birthday, in the coziest clean clothes I had and sleeping. In most cases, sleep is not my friend but at some point, your subconscious hits a brick wall and you sleep so deep that you don't even dream: it's just black nothingness. As a sexual abuse victim, you pray for black nothingness because it is the best kind of sleep. You don't relive anything or see faces you wish you could forget; you just are.

While most are celebrating the milestone of 16, I was just existing. I did not want to talk to Stacy about what I had experienced with Stan or what I had gone through. I told her what I was comfortable with her knowing, which wasn't much.

She pushed, but I dug my heels in deep on that one. I did NOT want to talk about it, not with her, not my stepdad, not anyone. My step dad tried so hard to be supportive I just wasn't ready. Stacy however, pushed hard for the details of my assaults. Now, I did eventually come around to talking about things with my counselor, but even that it took time. This book is the first time I'm revealing the full details of MY story to anyone, including my spouse. I don't speak these words, but writing them has been far easier than talking about them.

October 4th, 2006, days after I got back home, and after my 16th birthday, I was taken to a medical center to be looked at and tested for any potential STDs that could have occurred during any of my assaults. The end goal was to just make sure I was ok. This included a pap smear, which was less than comfortable after the last several weeks. The medical staff was great though. They were so accommodating, and made sure all of the doctors and staff that I had to deal with were female, ensuring things were more comfortable for me. The first notable thing discovered during the doctor's exam was my cervix. It was so infected, due to lack of being clean and raped, that she couldn't touch it with a Q-Tip without it bleeding. Thankfully, that was an easy fix of antibiotics.

All testing came back negative for STDs, but then the doctor entered the room, sat down, and with a big sigh said, "We have to talk." She then blurted out the words, "Your pregnancy test came back positive." I instantly started to cry. I had repeatedly told the detention staff in Montana that I thought I was pregnant. I had been given three separate pregnancy tests and even the detention doctor cracked jokes and mocked me saying that I must be the Virgin Mary. I told him that I felt God was telling me I was pregnant with a boy. I knew something wasn't right, but I was ignored and laughed at. So three negative pregnancy tests later, it was confirmed. I was pregnant at 16 years old.

Stacy called to tell my stepdad, who at the time, was not allowed to remain in our home. My stepdad had never done anything wrong towards me, but due to the nature of my case, no men except for my little brother were allowed to be in the home. When she called him, he lost it. He did what I think any protective dad would have done. He took a gun and went to Stan's house and was getting ready to murder him. He would have succeeded had Stacy not called the police on him. The police stopped my stepdad at Stan's doorstep just feet from completing his plan. My step dad, who was really Dad in my eyes, had rules in life. You didn't mess with kids, animals or the elderly. He wasn't a large man, only standing about 5 foot 7 inches. He was a man that stood for right being right, and wrong being wrong. He wasn't a perfect man; he had his problems like we all do, but he did everything he could to try and protect me.

That day, my stepdad was booked into Cobb County jail for attempted murder. I know now that my dad felt immense guilt for years. It ate away at him so badly that he ended up having a psychotic break and was arrested during a flashback. He felt like he failed to protect me. I've never once blamed him for the decision of what others did. He was without a doubt the only man that attempted to protect me while I was young.

JUDGE STALEY

SUPERIOR COURT OF COBB COUNTY
ACCUSATION

WARRANT NO. 06W12127   NO.   **065895**

STATE OF GEORGIA
VS.
GREGORY TODD GIBSON

The Defendant hereby waives indictment and formal arraignment and pleads
_____, this _____ day of _____, 20____.

_____   _____
Defendant   Defendant's Attorney

                                             _____
                                             Assistant District Attorney

STATE OF GEORGIA, COBB COUNTY

IN THE SUPERIOR COURT OF COBB COUNTY

I, PATRICK H. HEAD, the undersigned prosecuting attorney for the Superior Court of
Cobb County, on behalf of the people of the State of Georgia, do hereby charge and
accuse GREGORY TODD GIBSON with the offense of CRIMINAL ATTEMPT, for
that the said accused, in the County of Cobb and State of Georgia, on the 4TH day of
OCTOBER, 2006, did unlawfully attempt to commit the crime of murder, in violation
of O.C.G.A. § 16-5-1, in that the accused did knowingly and intentionally perform an
act which constituted a substantial step toward the commission of said crime, to wit:
having stated his intent to kill ███████████, said accused did then travel from his
residence in Griffin, Georgia, to the residence of ██████████ with a loaded
handgun concealed under a blanket and pillow on the passenger's seat of his vehicle;
contrary to the laws of said State, the good order, peace and dignity thereof.

Chapter 16

Is Abortion an Option?

Stacy's first response was, "Is abortion an option for you?" Absolutely 100% NO. My time in the juvenile detention center was spent reading a Bible. In no way could I morally do that. That is a monumental choice and not one I could make personally. In the Bible, it says what the devil uses for evil, the Lord can use for good (Genesis 50:20). I saw this child that I was carrying as a blessing, even if the circumstances in which he was conceived were not of love. This baby was meant to be here, regardless of the circumstances. I still, to this day, do not regret that decision and I still stand by it. The love I have for that child will never falter.

While Stacy never pushed the issue of abortion again after that, the question alone should have been my first clue, this child was not wanted in her household. Everything was still so fresh and new. Investigations were not complete; I had several interviews with police, for child victims', and it was just a crazy time all the way around. I also started seeing a counselor within the next few days and the appointments between everything were endless. Those days are also a haze. All the while, my dad still sat in jail, being held without bond at that time.

The first days home were difficult. I was adjusting to a new and different life, being pregnant, facing issues, and admitting bad things had actually happened to me. I chose to give up high school due to the pregnancy and pursue a GED. During the evenings, I would attend classes at the local technical college in preparation for taking my GED test. I had planned to take it and try to pass before the baby was born. I got a driver's license so I could get myself to the technical college and counseling appointments. I had to have Medicaid for my pregnancy, and I got involved with a pregnancy center that really coached me on my spiritual journey.

This is where God used the most amazing woman at exactly the perfect time.. Luci, who I am honored to call a friend, helped me through my pregnancy, counseled me through tough times, and really was the first person to instill a foundation of God and His love for me in my life. I was trying to adjust to so much that bouts of depression were easy to slip into. I met with Luci weekly as she talked to me about how God was working in my life and would continue to do so. She gave me pregnancy clothes when the time came and she mentored me all the way through my pregnancy. She carries Ruth-like qualities with unwavering faith, bravery, and always believing God will provide. Not only is she a stunning lady, but her soul cascades the love of Jesus into people and serving others. She's truly remarkable and God has and continues to use her in powerful ways.

All in all, I had a balancing act on my plate and was walking a tightrope. While I had a ton with which to keep up, in many ways it was good for me. It kept my mind busy. It kept my thoughts from wondering and from the fear of what was to come. The storm was not over. It was still brewing. I still had the biggest monster of all to deal with.... Stan. It was both frustrating and hard for me to deal with that. I had to tell my story and what happened a million and one times. I knew law enforcement was working, but it wasn't coming at a fast rate. I am not patient, I get anxious, and want/need things done now. Jesus is still working on my patience. I wanted "quick, fast, and in a hurry" out of fear, but these types of investigations take time. Every passing moment the monster was free was a moment I lived in fear. There was no easy escape, nowhere to hide, and certainly nowhere to run to. I was a sitting duck. A lamb ready for slaughter in a manner of speaking. I tried desperately to remember what Luci was teaching me about God's timing and trusting in Him, but my fear could be crippling at times.

While visiting the pregnancy center and seeking guidance there, I started attending a church. I had surrounded myself with amazing people, but it did not take the pressures of everyday life away. While the wisdom of the ladies who took me under their wings helped me tremendously, I still had a lot of decisions ahead of me and I still had more hardships ahead. Some days they felt impossible and some days I had hope. Either way, quitting wasn't optional for me.

Chapter 17

The Decision Made for Me

At some point, my dad was finally released from jail and the attempted murder charges were dropped. I don't remember how far along in my pregnancy that was, but he was also finally cleared to come back to the home. He was released on bond and given probation (see legal documents at the end of the chapter).

I wish I could tell you the date this all happened, but when asked what my plans were for the baby, I was slightly baffled. I wanted to keep the baby. I was told by both Stacy and dad that if I chose to keep the baby that I would be homeless. I'm unclear of whose decision that was. Stacy questioned abortion immediately. This leads me to believe that SHE did not want the baby in the house.

I was given no option to work and try to care for the baby myself. I was young with very little education but I was working on it. Still, they were adamant that my baby, my flesh and blood, would not be welcomed into their home.

I had just been away from my home for weeks, so I was scared to be away from my home. One could argue I chose to leave myself, which in part is true however, I did ask to be taken back home on more than one occasion. I wanted to be home. In counseling, I was dealing with the grooming portion of my therapy and understanding exactly how I had been manipulated.

I was accepting my mess-ups and I still do to this day. But now I was faced with an even deeper loss: the giving up of my own child at the threat of homelessness. I wouldn't consider myself a selfish person, but to put both myself and my child on the streets all because I loved and wanted him, would have been selfish and it was not a life I wanted for my baby.

With forced choices being put on me, I chose adoption. I do not regret my decision for my baby. I gave my baby a life I could not have otherwise, provided being so young and uneducated. The decision was made and the search for an adoptive family was on. I spoke to strangers on the phone and all of them were so nice and so deserving of a child, it was impossible to pick. This was the point I had to think of myself. If I were keeping this child, what kind of life would I want to provide? This led to many questions, phone calls, picture exchanges, and bios from families lining up in hopes to be chosen to be parents for my baby. It was both beautiful and discouraging. I would end up crushing someone trying to find my baby the perfect family.

The weight was overbearing, especially when it was not what I wanted at that time anyway. Crying became a regular part of my daily routine as I lived everyday with the acceptance that my time with my baby would be limited to me carrying him. I was sick in my first trimester, which made things slightly harder. Everything was changing. My body was changing, my plans for life, everything. Life always brings changes, but mine felt like they were moving at the speed of sound. I carried the heavy burdens of dealing with trauma on top of needing to choose a family for the baby I carried. I had good days and bad days, but everyday was filled with the unknown of what would happen.

I was still waiting for action on my case and that wait seemed to drag on forever, but I knew the detective on my case wasn't going to quit. I recognized that the day I met him.

IN THE SUPERIOR COURT OF COBB COUNTY, GEORGIA

Filed In Office Mar-20-2007 16:50:49
ID# 2007-0043014-CR
Page 1

CRIMINAL ACTION NO. 07-1508
WARRANT NO. 06101121217

Jay C. Stephenson
Clerk of Superior Court Cobb County

The State

vs

Gregory Todd Gibson

OFFENSE(S)

1-Carrying a concealed weapon

☑ PLEA ☐ NON-JURY ☐ JURY ☐ VERDICT
☑ NEGOTIATED ☐ GUILTY ON ☐ OTHER DISPOSITION
☑ GUILTY ON COUNT(S) 1 COUNT(S) ☐ NOLLE PROSEQUI ORDER ON
☐ NOLO CONTENDERE ON ☐ NOT GUILTY ON COUNT(S)
COUNT(S) COUNT(S) ☐ DEAD DOCKET ORDER ON
☐ TO LESSER INCLUDED ☐ GUILTY OF LESSER INCLUDED COUNT(S)
OFFENSE(S) ON COUNT(S) ☐ MERGED COUNT(S)

☐ FELONY SENTENCE ☑ MISDEMEANOR SENTENCE

WHEREAS, the above-named defendant has been found guilty of the above-stated offense, WHEREUPON, it is ordered and adjudged by the Court that the said defendant hereby sentenced to confinement for a period of 2 months

in the State Penal System or such other institution as the Commission of the State Department of Corrections or Court may direct, to be computed as provided by law. HOWEVER, it is further ordered by the Court

☑ 1) THAT the above sentence may be served on probation
☐ 2) THAT upon service of
PROVIDED that the said defendant complies with the following general and other conditions herein imposed by the Court as part of this sentence

☑ 1) Do not violate the criminal laws of any governmental unit.
☑ 2) Avoid injurious and vicious habits-especially alcoholic consumption/intoxication and narcotics and other dangerous drugs unless prescribed lawfully.
☑ 3) Avoid persons or places of disreputable or harmful character.
☑ 4) Report to the Probation-Parole Supervisor as directed and permit such Supervisor to visit him (her) at home or elsewhere.
☑ 5) Work faithfully at suitable employment insofar as may be possible.
☑ 6) Do not change his (her) present place of abode, move outside the jurisdiction of the Court, or leave the State for any period of time without prior permission of the Probation Supervisor.
☑ 7) Support his (her) dependents to the best of his (her) ability.

_____ 5% Victim Assistance Surcharge pursuant to O.C.G.A. 15-21-131
_____ 10% Jail Surcharge pursuant to O.C.G.A. 15-21-93
_____ DUI Surcharge pursuant to O.C.G.A. 15-21-112
_____ Per Month Probation Fee not to exceed 50 payments
_____ $50 or 10% bond or whichever is less pursuant to O.C.G.A. 15-21-73 (a)(1)(A)
_____ Probation Surcharge pursuant to O.C.G.A. 42-8-34 / 16-21 A-6
_____ 10% POPDF of original fine pursuant to O.C.G.A. 15-21-73 (e)(1)(B)
_____ 10% Brain and Spinal Injury Trust Fund pursuant to O.C.G.A. 15-21-149
_____ 5% of original fine for GA. Driver's Education Commission pursuant to O.C.G.A. 15-21-179
_____ 50% Drug Surcharge pursuant to O.C.G.A. 15-21-100
_____ $500 Court Costs pursuant to O.C.G.A. 15-6-77(h) (7)

IT IS FURTHER ORDERED that the defendant pay a fine in the amount of _____ and pay victim restitution in the amount of _____ and restitution to the Cobb General Fund for costs for Court-Appointed Attorney in the amount not to exceed _____ Defendant to be one of these penalties and restitution as a condition of probation at the rate of $ _____ per month beginning _____ days from _____

SEE ADDENDUM "A" FOR SPECIAL CONDITIONS OF PROBATION

IT IS THE FURTHER ORDER of the Court, and the defendant is hereby advised that the Court may, at any time, revoke any conditions of this probation and/or discharge the defendant from probation. The probationer shall be subject to arrest for violation of any condition of probation herein granted. If such probation is revoked, the Court may order the execution of the sentence which was originally imposed or any portion thereof in the manner provided by law after deducting therefrom the amount of time the defendant has served on probation.

The defendant was represented by the Honorable _Harlan Wood for Thomas_ Attorney at Law, _Fulton_ County, by ☐ (Employment) ☐ (Appointment)

Reported By _Alison Jordan_ _____ By the Court _____ 20 ___

So ordered this _30th_ day of _March_ 20 _07_

Defendant _____ Judge, Cobb Superior Court _Mary Staley_

STATE v GIBSON GREGORY TODD

Judge: STALEY CLARK

Filing Date: 11/30/2006

Prosecutor: DAWSON, SANDRA

Defendants	Pleadings	Hearings	Attorneys	Offenses	Appeals	Bond Information	Sentences

Def #	Count	Add Date	Bond Amount	Bondsman	Status	Bondsman Address
1	1	12/01/2006	$11,100.00	ALL COBB BAIL BONDING	ACTIVE	
1	2	12/01/2006	$11,100.00	ALL COBB BAIL BONDING	ACTIVE	

Chapter 18

The Waiting Game

One of the major interviews I had to do was a child victims' interview. I remember my detective so well. He was a man on a mission. You could see from the first meeting, he took what he did very seriously, and he did it with every bit of determination for the victims. He is what I like to refer to as the garbage man: he took out trash. I remember vividly the first time I met with him. It was a somewhat small room, with childlike paintings on the wall to make young children more comfortable. I was put in the room alone. I'm assuming that I was observed, but I don't know that for sure. After a short time, this particular detective we'll call John came in. He asked me several questions regarding Stan and the sexual assaults I had endured. I had to walk him through stories of Stan coming into the bottom story of the house and unlocking my door all hours of the night. I had to use proper vocabulary about things such as penis, vagina, penetration. It was obscenely uncomfortable. It had taken long enough to get semi-comfortable with a counselor, much less some male detective I didn't know. I took it all in stride, the best way I knew how, because I knew he was trying to help me.

The most important question of the interview was, "Are you willing to take a polygraph?" My answer was: of course, hook me up now. Tell me when to be here. I wasn't lying, in fact I've never lied about the things done to me. Or the things I've seen done to others. I had nothing to lose, so why lie? I had no reason to, but I know some will read this and doubt me. That is ok, sometimes the easiest truths are the hardest to swallow. I think Detective John believed me. According to Stacy, he said he knew I was telling the truth because you can't make up those details and that I was so willing to do the polygraph. Stan however, from what I hear, refused the test. I often wonder why? He did say "he was crazy enough to do it and he was crazy enough to go down for it."

Those were his exact words to me. I guess he changed his mind.

As we predicted, Stan went on the run. I completely understand that the police must have ducks in a row. As the movie *Law Abiding Citizen* said, "it's not what you know, it's what you can prove in court." It is not enough to know you've got a criminal; you have to have enough to get the warrants. By the time warrants for Stan were able to be obtained, he was on the run and nowhere to be found. Not only him, but Stan's wife and my brothers. This made the case more interesting because now law enforcement was pursuing a man on the run. We knew he would run, which made the situation far more complex. It's hard to take someone to court when you have no clue where to find them. Not only did it make it more complex, but it also made the situation scary. You do not know what someone is capable of when their backs are against the wall. They become unpredictable and that alone is what makes them scary. I knew it would be a matter of time before he was found. It wasn't an "if" but a "when." And when it happened what would he do? Would he try to hurt himself? Hurt law enforcement? Hurt one of my brothers? I would like to say I didn't have those thoughts but he had hurt me so I knew he was capable of just about anything.

This is just one of the news articles I could find all these years later. This was the beginning of an 18 month manhunt for Stan.

Mother pleads for safe return of kidnapped son

10:42 PM CST on Tuesday, January 23, 2007

By Wendell Edwards / 11 News

An Atlanta mother is pleading for the safe return of her son.

The last time ███████████ mother saw him, he was with his father, But police allege ███████ has since kidnapped his own son, and they say the boy could be in danger.

According to police, ███████████ 35, said he was going to return his son to Georgia from Virginia in November. But that never happened.

Instead police say they found ████████ abandoned pickup truck – along with a child safety seat and clothes – here in Houston, three days before Christmas.

"I'm here to plead that if you have any information whatsoever, that you please call to help bring ████████ home safely," ██████ s mother, ████████ ████████, said.

Authorities say ████████████ is also wanted on Aggravated Child Molestation and Incest and Deprivation charges in a separate case not involving his son.

████████ is described as a 5-year-old boy with red hair and blue eyes.

████████████ is described as 6'1" with brown hair and blue eyes. Police say that ████████ may have a mustache or beard and is known to work in or frequent adult entertainment businesses.

Anyone with information on the case is urged to contact police immediately."

Chapter 19

The Pregnancy and Birth

Nothing can ever prepare you to give up on
someone or something you love. I was given an
ultimatum. This decision weighed heavily on me.
Keeping my baby meant homelessness and a life of
struggle with no support. That's no life an
innocent baby should have to live. It was not an
easy decision for me, but it was a decision that had
to be made. As my pregnancy progressed and the
feel of flutters filled my womb, the choice became
harder to make. With every passing week and
every new kick, I felt this choice become a burden.
I loved this sweet, precious, innocent baby growing
inside me but I also knew I could not give him the
life he deserved.

I was sixteen, I had no money, no job and
very little education. What did I have to offer this
child other than love? I had so much love filled in
my heart for my baby, but love alone could not

raise and support him. I had to give him the life he deserved. That's right, I was carrying a sweet baby boy. He deserved better than I could give him and I wanted him to have more in life than I did. I had reluctantly made my decision. I did choose to keep him in my family. I had an aunt and uncle who longed for a child and it was the perfect fit. I could watch my sweet boy grow up from afar but also know he was always taken care of. It was the perfect fit for a hard situation.

It was decided my baby boy would be adopted at birth and my son would ultimately become my cousin. At this point my aunt and uncle became involved with finding an adoption attorney and setting everything in place for my baby boy to leave me and go home with them. I remember going to the attorney's office and discussing the agreements on the adoption. I was asked if I wanted money for him and I was baffled. I did not want money. I was not in some weird black-market world trying to sell my baby. I just wanted him to be loved and have an amazing family and the life I never had. I wanted the best for him and I still do to this day. The only thing I ever asked for was pictures of my baby boy growing up and to this day, almost sixteen years later, I've never received one from them. Some people might say that sentence sounds bitter but I hold no grudges towards my aunt and uncle. I do wish they could understand that I never decided on adoption because I didn't want him, I made the choice out of love and wanting him to have the best.

Luci and the women of the church celebrated my selflessness and threw me a celebration of life party. I wouldn't get to have a baby shower, this was a beautiful way for them to show their love for me. I was showered with more love than I was worthy of or deserved. Not one of the ladies in the room that day knew my decision for adoption had been a decision pushed on me. But I smiled, I laughed and I loved everyone. They saw something I didn't back then. I was broken garbage with no hope for the future. They saw the redeemed version of me. They saw the chains gone and they saw what God could do in my life even if I didn't see it yet. They saw my worth.

Finally, at forty one weeks and two days, I was sent to the hospital to be induced for labor. I was unable to dilate on my own, the Doctors and

nurses tried everything they could to progress
labor but nothing was working. I was feeling every
bit of the contractions and discomfort but my body
just wasn't doing what it needed to. I was tired,
hungry, uncomfortable and frustrated with the lack
of progress throughout labor. For thirty-three
hours they made every attempt to get some sort of
progression but nothing was working. My mucus
plug was stripped by hand by the most insensitive
mid-wife I've ever had the horror of experiencing. I
just gone through rape, incest, a kidnapping and a
pregnancy and this mid-wife treated me like I
deserved every bit of it.When she stripped my
mucus plug, she was not gentle about it at all. At
that point I was in tears and begging for a
C-section.

The nurse who took care of me that
morning was aware of what I had just been
through and knew the plan of adoption. She also
had been informed that throughout my pregnancy
I did successfully manage to complete and pass my
GED and was due to graduate in four days. Not
only was I graduating, I was being presented with
the President's Award for Educational Excellence.
After sacrificing so much for everyone else, this

was important to me and I wanted to make my graduation. She went to the midwife, who had just treated me with disdain, and begged her to give me the C-section. The midwife entered my hospital room minutes later with a look of disgust and judgment, and informed me that she would grant the C-section but she was listing it in my chart as AMA (against medical advice). Then she looked at the tray in front of me, which the hospital staff had delivered just minutes before, and with a sneer on her face told me I would have to wait another twelve hours because I had taken a few bites of Jell-o. I was beyond frustrated with this lady. It literally felt like she was doing everything she could to torture me. She didn't want to help me. I'm not sure if it was because I was a teen and she was "teaching me a lesson" or if she was disgusted by the fact that I had been a victim of sexual assault. Either way, she saw me as the scum of the earth which made an already difficult situation that much harder.

Finally, it was time for my C-section and while I had been poked, prodded, and treated horribly by the one midwife, I was thankful that I was made to wait that twelve hours because an angel delivered my boy: Dr. Killebrew. I remember her so vividly with her kind and compassionate blue eyes, coming to my bedside after I had been given my spinal block, and her telling me that she heard about what happened to me and she respected my strength in giving my boy life and a family. I never got to see more than her eyes because of the mask that covered her face for surgery, but I didn't need to. I laid there scared. I had never had a baby or a C-section and I was terrified. I felt lots of pressure and jerking. I threw up a few times while lying on the table and finally, I heard Dr. Killebrew say, "Wow, what a big boy" and I heard him cry. Even typing this now, brings tears to my eyes remembering that moment.

The doctor peeped her head around the curtain and said, "Good call on asking for the c-section, he would have never been born naturally." Apparently, I was so small and he was so big that as he attempted to turn head down, he got his head lodged in my hip. That's why I wasn't dilating, his heart rate kept dropping, and why I kept feeling so much pain in my hip. But he was here, and he was a healthy eight pound seven ounce bundle of perfection.

Chapter 20

The Aftermath

I was still open and on the surgery table when I was asked if I wanted to see him. Of course, I wanted to see him. I know Dr. Killebrew was just making sure I was okay with it out of respect. She treated me like a person. The nurse brought this perfect little boy to my bedside and he was handed off to Stacy. He was perfect. He looked like me. I remember reaching out and touching his cheek with tears forming in my eyes, knowing that this moment would not last long. I was days away from not seeing him for a very long time, possibly forever. Dr. Killebrew did just as she had promised. My baby boy was delivered perfectly healthy and months after my C-section, you could not even tell I had a C-section. Not only did Dr. Killebrew possess an amazing talent in delivery, but she treated me like a person. She spoke so gently and lovingly to that scared and broken sixteen year old girl. She never said but I believe she saw my brokenness and I believe she knew the sacrifice I was making in choosing to carry a baby, I knew I would never take home with me. I'd like to believe she felt a level of both sympathy for my situation and respect for the fact that I was attempting to be so selfless. Somehow, her very presence in the operating room made things feel peaceful and relaxing. I'm sure it was the kindness she showed me. I never got to see her full face but she had the most serene and calming light blue eyes I had ever seen. I am not sure why her eyes stay with me. Maybe it's because they say "the eyes are the window to the soul" and I saw a kind soul. But Dr. Killebrew, with her kind eyes and loving words, has stuck with me to this day.

But still I made the hardest decision I had yet. I chose not to hold my first baby boy. I didn't make this choice because I had any ill feelings towards this beautiful, perfect little being. I made that decision because If I put my arms around him, I would have never let go and I knew that the moment I saw him. I made so many promises to my aunt and uncle. I wanted to be selfish so badly. I wanted to hold him, love him, change a diaper. I wanted to be his mom, but I knew I was setting us both up for failure if I focused on my selfish wants.

The more I tried to be strong and not break, the more I felt I was being tested even more. When I got back to my actual room after surgery, I was met by my stepdad, a detective who had to take a DNA swab from both me and the baby, a nurse, a notary, and several other people who I can't remember. I was all jittery and itchy from the spinal block, which apparently is a normal reaction. I itched so bad, I left claw marks in my skin. I could not have any sort of pain medication until the adoption papers were signed. I had to be in a sound state of mind - not under the influence of any prescription drugs. And if I recall correctly, they had to be signed and notarized before midnight on the night he was born. I was already doing something I didn't want. Add exhaustion, hunger, pain, a medical reaction to the spinal block, and being completely overwhelmed with people and PTSD: that's a recipe for a complete shutdown. I didn't read one line of those adoption papers. I turned to the last page where my signature was required and I signed them so I could mourn my loss and block it all out. I was a completely demoralized sixteen year old girl, coerced into doing something I didn't want to. Shutting down was the easiest option and at the time, it seemed like the only option.

Hospitals are not the place for rest. The constant barrage of nurses and doctors that come in and out of the room leave you wanting nothing more than to leave. The beds are not built for comfort and it's near impossible to get comfortable after a C-section anyway. You cannot cough, laugh, sneeze, potty, or pass gas without feeling like you are going to bust the stitches and come apart completely. It is a miserable existence and hard on the body. Then, twelve hours after having laid on a table and being cut open, while completely awake and aware, with your intestines laid on a table, the hospital staff will ask you to get up and walk. You are drugged from pain meds with a feeling of cognitive dysfunction. Your head feels heavy in a sense, and you walk like the Hunchback of Notre Dame. That posture and gait are what I like to call the "C-section shuffle." Any attempt to stand up straight is met with failure, as the pain of those first days is so intense. Day three after C-section was the hardest, but walking and movement kept the muscles from getting stiff, which kept the pain at tolerable levels. The day after the baby was born, I gathered my vigor (both mentally and physically) and walked to the nursery to see him through a piece of glass. That moment of seeing my aunt hold him up so I could see him was the last moment I physically saw him in person. He was a day old. I was not his mom anymore. Not for lack of wanting to be, but by coercion and legal paperwork. I no longer had any rights to this beautiful human my body created.

Letting go was hard enough, but having to fill out a birth certificate for a baby you would never take home felt like affliction. I was thankful for pain meds, at least it made me somewhat desensitized to the situation. I know that sounds terrible, but I'm not sure I would have made it through the situation otherwise. I was mourning a loss. No, my baby boy did not die, but it was still a loss. And it still mutilated me internally. I had to mentally place myself in a state of disassociation to get through those few days. My aunt and uncle went home with a baby and I went home with a vacant womb and aimless arms. Although I had spent months preparing for those moments in counseling, nothing really prepares you for that loss. A mother's instinct will kick in as it's supposed to. I felt like I couldn't speak up for myself because that ultimately meant the worst life possible for us. The choice was the right choice, but it didn't make the hurt go away.

My only regret to this day was never taking a moment and holding my son. At that moment, I made that choice because I feared I wouldn't let go, and that was a real possibility. My now thirty-two year old self understands I will never be able to go back and hold that tiny human that I had just spent months growing inside me. I will never get that time back and he'll never be little again. My decision to not hold him is one that continues to bother me, even if at that moment it may have been the best decision. I went home to the only thing in the world I felt like I had left. My dog.

During my pregnancy Stacy and Dad
(stepdad but that man was my dad) got me a puppy
from the pound. She chose me. She was my heart
dog. As soon as I opened the kennel, she ran
straight to me. She chose me. I named her Bailey,
and she was the only thing in the world that
depended on me. She became my best friend and in
a lot of ways she saved me from myself.

So, I went home to Bailey. My first days
home were spent on a couch. Not because I didn't
have a bed, but because it was the easiest place to
get comfortable trying to endure the pain. Stacy
took me to a thrift store to buy me a dress for my
graduation. It was pretty much the only thing I
could look forward to at that moment. I graduated
in my thrift store dress and afterwards celebrated
the accomplishment at the local Mexican
restaurant. I didn't really have friends in those
days. I was sixteen and surrounded by adults
constantly. I didn't go out, I kept to myself. Most
kids my age were in high school, but I was getting
ready to start college. After the baby was born, I

was offered a job working as a lawyer's assistant because I had an interest in law. I worked there for several months, three days a week. I eventually left, not because I didn't enjoy the work, but because the travel was far and I needed more than three days' worth of work. Not long after this, my dad left for Iraq around 2008. He voluntarily went over as a civilian contractor for KBR to drive a truck.

Dad had a military background but he and Stacy didn't marry until I was thirteen years old, so I had never had to experience someone leaving to go to a war zone. I have so much respect for those who serve our country. My dad was leaving voluntarily, there are some who don't get that choice. It is so hard to drop someone you love and care about off at an airport knowing they are going to be half a world away from you. It's not easy on the household or on the one leaving.

I started classes at the local community college. Initially it was in paralegal studies, but I had no clue of what I really wanted to do. I was sixteen and I did not have life figured out. I went to work at McDonald's as a cashier. It was close to the house, so gas was minimal, and I got hours. It wasn't the best job, but it paid my bills and kept me from sitting at home and going stir crazy. I needed something to do so I did not have to relive and remember my past. I started to have anxiety, but I never dealt with it the way I should have. Instead, I picked up smoking. It's such a bad habit. I wish now I would have never touched a cigarette. It does not take any of my stress or anxiety away, it just adds to health problems. I worked at McDonald's for a long time, and I met a cook there who I became friends with.

We will call him Jim. I should have known Jim was trouble. He was being brought to work everyday by a work release program because he had just gotten out of jail. He was also ten years older than I was. But for some reason, in my state of self-sabotage, I fell for what seemed like a nice guy image. I still did not think I was worthy of much, so I didn't set a standard for myself when it came to dating. In the brokenness I was in, I shouldn't have been looking to date at all, but I suppose I was trying to fill a void somehow. Jim had an issue with drugs, claiming he had gotten clean while incarcerated. I believed him. And at the time we started talking, he was clean and doing well. Of course, neither of us had dream jobs, but we had jobs and we got close quickly. I was headed for more years of hurt and abuse and it was clothed in the impersonation of love.

Chapter 21

The Path to Self-Destruction

I don't know what I was thinking in finding someone not only ten years older than me, but also someone who had just gotten out of jail. Now that's not to say that people cannot change or that because someone has been to jail that they are bad people. Anyone can be redeemed, but I knew that Jim had a history with drugs and theft which is not the most desirable characteristic of a partner in life. Yet, I still put myself in that position. I desired to feel something so badly other than hurt that I definitely didn't care where or whom it came from. That is still a pretty sad existence: so broken you'll just accept anything regardless of how bad it is for you.

At first it wasn't all bad. As we got to know each other, we enjoyed our time working together. We bonded over a love of music, hung out during breaks at work, and just overall enjoyed each other's company while at work. At this time, he was only allowed to be released when he was working, so there wasn't any going out or hanging out beyond our shifts together.

Eventually, Jim did get released from his work release program and moved in with his grandmother. I visited him the day he got "home" and this was when our relationship started to turn from nothing more than friends and coworkers to an actual relationship. Again, it wasn't all bad at first. We enjoyed hanging out and getting to know one another. I brought him around my house. He met Stacy and obviously we were in a relationship. I was seventeen at the time and Jim was ten years older than me. Looking back now I really don't know what I saw good for myself in that relationship. When I say that, I don't mean to sound selfish, but in life you want people who build you up and make you better, not bring you down. I rushed into a relationship for the sake of having one. Even Stacy supported the relationship enough that she paid for the engagement ring that Jim presented to me at the Moose Lodge bar proposal during karaoke. I'm not sure if this was an attempt for her to get rid of me, so I wouldn't be under her roof any more, or if her standards were just that low but she had no problem accepting a recovering drug addict convicted felon, ten years my senior, who was already married, as my future mate.

To make my standards lower than they already were, my "fiance" was still legally married to someone else. Now they were not together at all, but Lord what was I thinking? I'm not a person of judgment because I am so perfectly imperfect. I don't dare consider myself worthy of the life I have today, but I stepped into an already chaotic situation. Jim had two small children. I grew to love those kids, but it was far more complicated than what meets the eye. See Jim and his wife ("ex-wife" who he was still legally married to) both had drug issues and neither had custody of the kids. Jim's grandmother had custody. Those poor kids had more than their fair share of odds stacked against them as well. I tried desperately to love them, but was often met with defiance because "I was not their mom" or "I wasn't the boss." They were very smart kids who were funny and were so fun to be around, but not one adult had taught them right and wrong, or that their actions had consequences. When I did try, I was met with anger and contempt from members of Jim's family. Not one person cared how those children acted. Jim eventually fell off the wagon, went back to crack, and was sent back to jail. He wasn't there very long, but was ordered to attend drug classes to help him. He did end up getting clean again and we were able to save our relationship, at least for the time being. I thought I was head over heels in love with Jim but I STILL didn't know what it meant to be loved.

Chapter 22

Spy Guy and the Extradition

During this time, Stan had still been on the run and was wanted by the FBI; not only for incest, but also for the kidnapping of my little brother. Now, to be fair to Stan, I do not know what the custody arrangement was between Stan and my little brother's mother. Those records were sealed upon my research. We do not share the same biological mother, so I can't say with certainty anything on that matter. I have heard he wasn't kidnapped, but at the same time, why would the FBI be pursuing him? Also why run, and why dump your vehicle? These are things that just make the puzzle impossible to piece together. This story is crazy enough, but I myself have been left with more questions than answers over the years.

For eighteen months we waited: not knowing their location, if my brother was alright, anything for that matter. They had basically disappeared without a trace, that was until a very talented guy stepped into the picture. His name is Jake Schimdt. He is a spy. He makes men in black look like a joke. Jake is a self-described "gumshoe" with a talent for finding anyone. He's quoted as saying, "There are about **65,000** kidnapped children per year and I can find them in **30** days, or I will retire. I've done it before and will continue to." Jake is tall, with slicked-back jet black hair and the coolest fu manchu I've ever seen. Crisp and clean in his appearance, you'd never guess a spy but I guess that's part of the hunt. You could place him in Vegas and he'd easily be mistaken as a high roller and not a spy, out to hunt prey. He is not the spy you see in Hollywood films. He is of his own breed. He makes Hollywood spies look like play school. Infamously, known to be security for a number of stars, he uses his talents to help find missing children.

I'm not one hundred percent sure how Jake got my brother's case, but he did. True to his word, he found him in two weeks. Using his own time, money, knowledge, and resources, Stan was finally being extradited back to Georgia from Mexico to await trial and face his charges in front of a jury of his peers.

I don't think any of this would have been possible without the knowledge and expertise of Jake Schmidt. The coolest and most dedicated spy guy I have the pleasure of knowing. He's the real deal and I'm honored to call him my friend.

CERTIFICATE OF INDIGENCY
IN THE SUPERIOR COURT FOR
THE COUNTY OF COBB STATE
OF GEORGIA

IN THE CASE OF:

THE STATE VS.

▬▬▬▬▬

Appointed Counsel:

KNIGHTON, RONNIE

Bar Number—>>>>>> 426600

WARRANT AND CASE SUMMARY INFORMATION

Warrant / Case Information	Date	Jail?	Add On?	Jurisdiction
2007W5371	06/08/2008	Yes	☐	Superior Court
2006W13758	06/08/2008	Yes	☐	Superior Court

Type	Warrant #	Case #	Charge Description	Notes
MIS	2006W13758		CNTRBUTE DELINQ MINR	
FEL	2006W13758		INCEST	
FEL	2006W13758		CHILD MOLEST/AGG CHM	
FEL	2007W5371		INTERFER W CUSTODY	

Nonetheless, it was time for me to face my biggest monster yet. I had to show up in court and face Stan. I had to say things I never wanted to repeat, but I had to if I stood any chance of facing my fear. I truly believe this was a power play by the defense, but I walked into the courtroom and was literally feet away from Stan. I was stopped to stand in front of him, as his attorney made some ridiculous motion. I had to stand there. Standing face to face with the man that had abused me for years. I was then asked to leave. They were not ready for me yet. It was a power play to scare me and it somewhat worked.

It's like calling a time out with seconds left in the game and hoping the kicker freezes on the winning field goal. Yes, I looked him in the face, but I was scared and I went into a state of disassociation. I was numb. When I got on the stand I was asked tons of questions. I answered matter of factly, but I could not bring myself to show any emotion. Just like counting cracks on the ceiling, I had left my own mind just to get through the court proceedings. Not only had I mentally gone back to a place of not feeling, I also didn't want to show Stan any emotion. I wanted to be strong and not give Stan the satisfaction of seeing me break. I got emotional one time on the stand, and it was when they brought up my son who I had given up for adoption. They knew that was a sensitive subject. It was not pertinent to the case against Stan and should have never been allowed. Stan doesn't like to play fair though, playing dirty is his game. I wasn't granted motions to limine to not disclose "private matters" like he was. I don't remember the questions or the responses. What mattered more to me was that I got through it.

Filed In Office Feb-01-2010 10:29:55
ID# 2010-0016915-CR
Page 1

Jay C. Stephenson
Clerk of Superior Court Cobb County

IN THE SUPERIOR COURT OF COBB COUNTY

STATE OF GEORGIA

THE STATE   )
)
-vs-   )
)
)

MOTION IN LIMINE

(1)

COMES NOW the Defendant and hereby moves the Court, in limine, to issue

an Order prohibiting the State from introducing any evidence, testimonial or

otherwise, that Defendant failed to come talk with the police when requested and fled

the State to avoid prosecution.

(2)

Defendant further moves the Court, in limine, to issue an Order prohibiting

the State from introducing any evidence alleging the Defendant being of bad

character and particularly from witness

JUDSON R. KNIGHTON
Ga. Bar No. 426600
Attorney for Defendant

P.O. Box 756
Marietta, Georgia 30061
770-428-8135

FILED IN COURT
2-1   20 10

JAY C. STEPHENSON
CLERK SUPERIOR COURT
COBB COUNTY GEORGIA

JUDGE ROBINSON

Jay C. Stephenson
of Superior Court Cobb County

GENERAL BILL OF INDICTMENT

083983

RE: Warrant(s)
06-W-13758

NO.

COBB SUPERIOR COURT

WITNESSES:
Det. McCraw
CCPD

STATE OF GEORGIA

JULY/AUGUST TERM 2009

THE STATE OF GEORGIA vs

True BILL   Date: 8-7-09   20 09

Delivered in open Court by

Grand Jury Foreperson   Grand Jury Bailiff

1776

JAY C. STEPHENSON, Clerk, S. C.

PATRICK H. HEAD,
District Attorney, Cobb Judicial Circuit

The Defendant herein waives copy of indictment, list of witnesses, formal arraignment and pleads NOT Guilty.	The Defendant herein waives copy of indictment, list of witnesses, formal arraignment and pleads _____ Guilty.
Defendant	Defendant
Attorney for Defendant	Attorney for Defendant
Assistant District Attorney	Assistant District Attorney

S

in the name and behalf of the citizens of Georgia, charge and accuse ▓▓▓▓▓ with the offense of **AGGRAVATED CHILD MOLESTATION** for that the said accused, in the County of Cobb and State of Georgia, on, or about the 14th day of January, 2005, did commit an immoral and indecent act to, with and in the presence of Ashley ▓▓▓▓ a child under the age of sixteen years, with the intent to arouse and satisfy the sexual desires of the accused by placing his mouth on her vagina; contrary to the laws of said state, the good order, peace and dignity thereof.

COUNT TWO

and the Grand Jurors, aforesaid, in the name and behalf of the citizens of Georgia, further charge and accuse ▓▓▓▓ with the offense of **AGGRAVATED CHILD MOLESTATION** for that the said accused, in the County of Cobb and State of Georgia, on, or about the 14th day of January, 2005, did commit an immoral and indecent act to, with and in the presence of Ashley ▓▓▓▓ a child under the age of sixteen years, with the intent to arouse and satisfy the sexual desires of the accused by allowing the child to place her mouth upon his penis; contrary to the laws of said state, the good order, peace and dignity thereof.

COUNT THREE

and the Grand Jurors, aforesaid, in the name and behalf of the citizens of Georgia, further charge and accuse ▓▓▓▓ with the offense of **INCEST** for that the said accused, in the County of Cobb and State of Georgia, on, or about the 14th day of January, 2005, did engage in sexual intercourse with his daughter, whom he knew he was related to by blood; contrary to the laws of said state, the good order, peace and dignity thereof.

Chapter 23

The Verdict

I managed to hold it together through court, but the verdict was a completely different story. Stan was charged with four felony counts: two were aggravated child molestation, one count of incest, and one count of statutory rape. The days came and went, and it felt like eyes were always one me. I had been raped and molested in 2004 and 2005. It was now 2010. I had some healing time and I had a great counselor, but it felt like I couldn't laugh or smile if we were out of court for lunch, because the eyes of the jury were constantly on me. They were watching to answer the question: "is she a real victim" or an actress? I knew I told the truth and I did not need to milk reactions for sympathy to prove it.

I was a very different person from the thirteen and fourteen year old me to the nearly twenty year old me. We were shuffled into the courtroom to await the verdict. And the verdict was read as follows:

We, the members of the jury, in regards to The State v. [redacted] do find the following:

As to Counts One and Two, aggravated child molestation - we, the jury, find the defendant - NOT GUILTY!!!!

At the time I couldn't believe it. Every fear of not being believed was coming true. Those words ringing in my ears just solidified to me why so many don't speak up and don't tell their stories. It's because we bear all the courage we can, only to be told we weren't "convincing" enough to find someone guilty. The victims carry the burden of being believed not the perpetrators.

As to Count Three, Incest, we the jury find the defendant - NOT GUILTY!!!!!

I collapsed into Stacy saying, "No, no, they got it wrong, they don't believe me."

As to Count Four, Statutory Rape, we the jury find the defendant - NOT GUILTY!!!!

On the last not guilty, I couldn't take it anymore. I RAN from the courtroom in tears. I couldn't believe what had just happened. Not only did the jury not believe me, but Stan would be free to go on and live his life as if none of this had ever happened. I got to carry the scars. I was angry with the jury for a long time. How could they get this so wrong? Why didn't they believe me?

Today I know why. This was a classic case of he said/she said. I had never kept any proof that Stan had touched me. Basically, there was reasonable doubt among the jury. Today as an adult, I can totally understand the decision in that verdict as I had no physical proof that anything had ever happened. I know it did and Stan knows it did. But, I eventually came to terms with the fact that he has to answer for that when he leaves this world.

I do not. I've forgiven him long ago, mainly because I can't change what happened. However, I'm not going to allow what happened to eat away at me and destroy the good I can put into this world. If I can help one person, my personal struggles have been for something.

IN THE SUPERIOR COURT FOR THE COBB JUDICIAL CIRCUIT

Jay C. Stephenson
Clerk of Superior Court Cobb County

STATE OF GEORGIA

THE STATE OF GEORGIA	§	CRIMINAL INDICTMENT
v.	§	
▇▇▇▇▇▇	§	▇▇▇▇▇▇

VERDICT

As to Count 1, Aggravated Child Molestation, we the jury, find the defendant, ▇▇▇

not guilty.

As to Count 2, Aggravated Child Molestation, we the jury, find the defendant, ▇▇▇

not guilty

As to Count 3, Incest, we the jury, find the defendant, ▇▇▇

not guilty

As to Count 4, Statutory Rape, we the jury, find the defendant, ▇▇▇

not guilty.

This the 8th day of February, 2010.

FILED IN COURT
2 - 8 20 10

JAY C. STEPHENSON
CLERK SUPERIOR
COBB COUNTY, GEORGIA

Foreperson (Signature)

Michael F. O'Neill
Foreperson (Print Name)

Chapter 24

Starting Over

Not long after Jim was released from jail, I told him I had plans to try to enter the Army. It was something Stacy was pushing, but also something I thought would be good for me. I had taken the ASVAB test once and missed passing by one point. I was set to take it again when I found out I was pregnant. Jim and I were gonna have a baby. I was honestly so happy. I felt like this was my chance to finally be a mom. I didn't really have a plan. I wasn't scared of being pregnant this time like I had been the first time. I knew I would be just fine and I'd do everything I could to protect this baby. I was extremely anxious that something would happen to this baby because I had been deprived of my first baby. I tried not to let that bother me. I tried to celebrate the fact that I was finally going to get the chance to hold my baby for the first time and be the mom I could have been the first time, had I been given the chance.

The celebration was short-lived. Not long into my pregnancy, I found out just how mean and abusive Jim could be. The first time he ever hurt me, he got angry at me. I don't recall why, it was probably something ridiculous, but he grabbed me aggressively by the arm and threw me out the back door, which caused me to fall and hit the back deck of our duplex. The neighbors saw what happened. The next morning the neighbor told me if he ever saw Jim do that again he was gonna call the police on him the next time. They moved shortly after that incident. Weeks later, Jim got so drunk he couldn't even stand up. I was pregnant and trying to help him up out of the bathroom floor and to the bed. He got angry with me and spit a loogie in my face. Jim then cracked a thick beer mug across my eyebrow so hard I thought he had split my eyebrow open. Thankfully, it was nothing more than some soreness and a slight bruise. I think the job I had was suspicious that something wasn't right with him and fired me shortly after.

I did manage to land a job at a Waffle House a little drive away. I was the only one working to ensure I had what I needed for our little boy. I was having another boy. I was working as much as I could, just to have money. At one point, I worked a twenty-one hour shift at six months pregnant trying to make ends meet. At home, Jim often laid in bed, drank, or played video games. I was doing my best to keep our heads above water. We had two roommates, but even that didn't cover all the expenses. Things with Jim's anger got so bad that he attempted to attack me one night while I was probably seven or eight months pregnant. Had it not been for the male roommate we had at the time, grabbing him and literally choking him out to the point of Jim passing out, who knows what would have happened to me that night.

Jim struggled with anything that involved addiction. If it was drugs he did them. If it was alcohol, he drank it. He was more focused on the way he felt than being a dad or a partner. But I stayed for the sake of the little boy I carried. When it came to naming him, Jim "let" me do it, because he knew what had happened with my first son. So he "allowed" me to name our son. Typing that now I can see the control. How I didn't see it then I don't know.

Chapter 25

The Boy who FINALLY Made Me a Mom

The day finally came on November 11th. I had to have another C-section. I checked into the hospital early. I want to say we had to be there at six in the morning. I was anxious and nervous. I couldn't wait to see what he would look like, how big he would be, to hold him for the first time, and snuggle him. It was everything I had waited on. I was, as they say, "large and in charge" but I had struggled throughout my pregnancy to gain weight. The hospital staff and my doctors had concerns that he would be small, which made me more nervous. I was literally "all belly" and I only gained twenty-five pounds my entire pregnancy. I hate hospitals as it is. There is something that feels cold and unwelcoming about them. I know it's where people go to be born and to die, but something about hospitals makes me feel more anxious than at peace. It's hard to describe. I got into my gown and waited as the clock ticked by. The hours felt like they were passing slower and slower. Operating rooms are never on time unless it's an emergency, so the hours dragged on. I made every attempt I could to find comfort to rest, but I was far too anxious to rest and was terribly hungry. I couldn't eat after midnight, so the baby and I were unhappy with the lack of food.

After what felt like forever, it was finally time. I walked to the OR, got on their table, and prepared for them to insert the needle in my spine to block all feeling so I could have my boy. Jim was not yet in the room. They prepared me first and brought him in next. The tough guy needed a chair because he was ghost white and ready to pass out. I guess he didn't realize I was the one practically being sawed in half. However, he joined me at my bedside and sat next to me as the hospital staff got started on delivering my baby boy. Finally, at 1:30 PM, he was here. My baby boy had entered this world perfectly healthy. He was a little on the smaller side as they predicted (at six pounds, two ounces), but he was here and healthy. That's all I could wish for. I was taken into recovery where I was monitored to make sure I was alright. The anxiety in me grew.

Subconsciously, I feared what had happened before. I was told to rest. I couldn't rest until I had my baby boy in my arms. When I got back to my room Jim, my roommates, and my grandmother were there - but no baby. I know the nursery had to be annoyed with me as I probably called them ten times in a few hours. They were giving my boy a bath and ensuring that his temperature and everything looked good. I didn't care. I wanted my boy with me and safe in my arms. The hospital staff had given me so many things to help me relax that they couldn't give me any more. If they did, they'd kill me. My doctor told me he had given far less medication to two hundred pound men and it knocked them out. This was further proof that you cannot do anything to stop a lioness from protecting her babies.

Finally, after hours of waiting, I had my boy wrapped safely in my arms and my entire world changed in a second. I don't know why but I had this overwhelming need to protect him. As a mother, we always want to protect our babies, but something irked me about my baby. He would need far more protection than what I had imagined. And I was correct. I named my boy Noah. God made a covenant with Noah. Just as He had His Son do for me. I was fearfully and wonderfully made, as was my boy. Noah just fit. It rained the day before, the day of, and the day after he was born. Animals of different kinds kept appearing in pairs of two throughout my pregnancy. God had blessed the name of Noah for my boy. I've jokingly said If I had not named him Noah, God would have struck me down.

The night of Noah's birth, I was left in the hospital room alone after my C-section, sick and vomiting from all the anesthesia, only for Jim, his ex-wife, and my roommates to go out and celebrate. Had it not been for the Pastor of my church at the time and his wife coming by to see me, I would have been alone. They didn't stay very long, so I was in the hospital unable to get up, while trying to take care of Noah alone. Jim came stumbling in sometime around one in the morning while we were trying to rest. I should have known at that moment that partying and having fun were a top priority to Jim. But I'd just had our baby boy and for all the things I didn't have as a child, I wanted Noah to have a family.

I was happy to be leaving the hospital with my baby boy for the first time. I was exhausted and ready to go home. I had a terrible reaction to the adhesive film they put across my back for them to do the spinal block. I had raised itchy hives all across my back that emulated dinosaur or elephant skin. It was painful and irritating on top of the pain of recovery. Of all of that, the worst part was the baby blues. I sunk into a slight postpartum depression, knowing that staying with Jim would only mean hardship for Noah and I. Merely by looking at Noah, I'd start crying knowing he deserved better and because he was so beautiful.

Noah became everything I lived for and I was the happiest I had ever been. I loved someone more than I could love myself. I came to the conclusion that I had to do better for Noah. I called Stacy and my dad. At the time, they were driving an 18-wheeler cross country for work. They were not able to make it home for Noah's birth, but they got to meet him about a week later. My dad instantly fell in love with Noah. Dad loved babies and they always seemed to flock to him. I asked to move in with them, as I had to do what was best for Noah. Of course, Jim told everyone that I was "taking his son from him." Noah and I were only twenty minutes away (the next county over) and I don't recall him being that concerned about "his son" when he left me in the hospital to go party the night Noah was born. That's old news and is nothing that can be changed now.

I moved in with Stacy and dad when Noah was just two weeks old. They helped me get "preemie" clothes for Noah because even though six pounds is a 'normal' birth weight, he was just a little guy. I was in a safe place to take care of Noah and they let me drive their pick-up truck if I needed to go to appointments or anything. They were back on the road and I was bored to death. I had no one around. I had no company, no friends, nothing. The only thing I could do was sit at the house and go stir crazy. Noah was just a tiny little baby, so he slept a lot which made the days go slower. Taking care of him was easy. He was a great baby that slept well and was happy. I just had nothing to do. No work, no friends, I wasn't in school, or working at the time, so the hours and days seemed to take longer to pass.

Occasionally, Jim would come by to see Noah or pick us up for dinner. This opened my relationship back up with Jim. I also missed my dog, Bailey, who Jim had at the time because Stacy and dad's location wouldn't allow pets. So even though we were not together, Jim knew how much Bailey meant to me and agreed to take care of her until I could get her back. This further pushed me back into the arms of Jim. After some time of him begging, I agreed to move back in with him. I thought it would be good for Noah to have us both and I was lonely. People with PTSD, anxiety, and depression will almost always choose what's bad for them if it means escaping the loneliness they feel.

I packed my things and moved out. Stacy and dad weren't terribly happy about it. I moved into a partially renovated home that Jim had been working on for a guy.. The place was a mess because of the renovations, but the room we stayed in allowed Noah to be with us and I had my "Boogie" (my nickname for Bailey) back. We stayed at that place for some time until we were offered a rent-to-own place with a little land by the guy Jim was doing renovations for.

Things seemed to be moving in a positive direction for us. We had a new place, Jim was clean, working, and we were raising Noah. Everything seemed to be falling into place. I enrolled in school to get an associate's degree to better support both myself and things for Noah. Things were looking up. But what goes up must come down.

Chapter 26

The Blowup and The End

The one thing I've learned about addicts is that they cannot involve themselves with people that are also addicts: they fall into the same traps too easily. The same vicious cycle continues to repeat itself and they spiral.

Unfortunately, this was the path Jim chose. He got a call from his friend saying that he needed some help with renovations on his house. Jim agreed to go help. We were supposed to stay there for renovations for only a couple of days, but it ended up being a couple of weeks. The women and children stayed in the already renovated house at the bottom of the hill and the men stayed up at the house on top of the hill that only had electricity. The problem was that not much was getting renovated because they all were too busy smoking pot and playing video games. What little time his friend did come down to the house was normally to abuse his own wife, which I heard on several different occasions.

Three weeks had passed when Noah came down with a fever. I told Jim we needed to go back to our own house and care for Noah. He agreed and said he would walk up the hill to the other house and let his friend know. After waiting in the car for almost an hour, I angrily stomped to the house up on the hill and found Jim smoking pot with his friend, having a great time, as our son sat in the car sick. Not only was I angry, but disgust filled me. How could a parent put getting high over their sick child? I told him I was leaving and taking Noah home with or without him. He got paid $100 for the three weeks we spent there. I was more than upset. I was just completely done with the chaos this life was producing. Jim got in the car and I had to rush back towards where we live, hoping to make it to the dollar store in time to grab just a few things for my sick baby. I didn't make it before they closed due to Jim's lack of awareness to the situation.

I was pretty fed up with the treatment that both me and Noah were receiving. I made a phone call to Jim's probation officer only to find out that Jim had not reported to his probation, and had an active warrant out for his arrest. He got angry, picked up my laptop that I had paid for to put myself through school, and shattered the entire thing. His end goal was to stop me from becoming my best self. Jim was desperately trying to hold me back so I didn't better myself and so he would always have control. Unfortunately for him, I insured the laptop and was able to rent another one from Aaron's for a few weeks to complete my assignments. He was not going to stop me from reaching my goals. Too much had been taken from me already.

I made a phone call to Jim's mother and told her he was wanted. If she did not come to get him at that moment, I would call the police and have him charged for destroying my property and for his warrants. He left quickly, mad at the fact that I had some control over the situation. I suppose Jim thought I would be angry for a little bit and "come to my senses" and just let him come back. I told him I didn't think that the relationship was good for either of us. It was toxic, abusive, and wouldn't continue. I allowed him to come over to discuss visitation and how he could help me financially with Noah. BIG MISTAKE!!!!!!

This invitation only brought more abuse and manipulation into my home. At first, the visit seemed cordial, trying his best to "smooth things over." When that didn't work, he asked me bluntly if I was seeing someone. I wasn't seeing anyone. I had hung out with an old friend recently and told Jim about it. Now, I did date this friend in middle school, however we were nothing more than friends. He told me he cared about me, but could not see anything more happening between us. He was not ready to step up and take on a kid. I totally respected and appreciated him for his honesty. Jim got so angry that I had a friend over, he smashed another laptop. That was the second laptop in a matter of six weeks. He cornered me at the front door. I had no way to get away from him or to reach Noah. Thankfully, Noah was preoccupied with Blue's Clues and his toys in his own room. I don't know what happened to me, but being cornered like that put me in a fight or flight mode. As he raised his fist to hit me, something in me just snapped. I drew my fist back and I struck him, catching him on the cheek first before he could ever lay that fist on me. I was liberated. I had finally fought back for once. I told him he had just raised his hand to me for the very last time. I am not proud that I hit someone. I am proud, however, that after so many years of abuse by so many people, I finally fought back and defended myself. Jim backed down once I stood up for myself. I have found that bullies often prey on those they believe they can control or are weaker. The minute you stand up for yourself and refuse to accept the abuse, they become cowards.

His mother came to pick him up again. I told him he would rent me a laptop until I could replace mine. I wasn't getting behind in school over his actions. He did rent the laptop, but only under the threat of me charging him. Not long after getting the laptop, maybe a couple of days later, he called and had all the power and water shut off on me and our son. It was another manipulation tactic, only wanting control, with no care for Noah or his well being. Thankfully, the guy that owned the house was more than willing to turn both back on in his name so that Noah and I would have what we needed until Stacy and dad could get home and get things switched over into their names. I was basically a single parent. I did not allow Jim to come to the home any more. All he brought was manipulation and abuse through my door. I did still allow him to get Noah every other weekend. He was also giving me $100 per week to help with whatever I needed for Noah. Stacy and dad were helping pay for daycare so I could work while they were on the road. In the evenings, I was doing school work and taking care of Noah by myself. I was one busy mama, but that sweet boy kept me going.

When Noah was eighteen months old, his pediatrician determined that he needed tubes; he was practically deaf due to fluid build-up around his ear drums. Jim did go to the hospital with me the day of Noah's surgery and it seemed like we were falling into a good co-parenting agreement. Things were not chaotic; they were as they should be for the most part. We may not have been a couple any more, but we still had a child together and working together for Noah's best interest would be crucial. Noah made it through surgery just fine. Eventually his speech began to improve, which was the reason for the surgery in the first place. His speech wasn't developing at all and he could not hear. If I called him, he wouldn't respond until I would stomp on the floor.

Jim finally called me one Friday in August and wanted to discuss further arrangements for Noah. I agreed to meet him, but only in a public place. I still refused to allow him at the house because I wasn't setting myself or Noah up for hurt any more. I got Noah a sitter for the night. I didn't want Jim to try anything silly. We met at a local place not far from my house on the town square. They often did karaoke on Friday nights, which I still enjoyed. He really didn't discuss anything more than what we already had in place. I believe this was a pitiful attempt to get me out so he could try to manipulate me back into a relationship.

My friend was the bartender at the location. I was only twenty years old, so obviously I didn't drink or anything. I went to the bar to say hey and chat with her for a minute. I sat next to the most obnoxiously drunk man in the entire place. Due to him acting out, I spoke with her for just a few minutes before heading back to our table, avoiding a scene because this guy was getting rowdy. This wasn't a typical "bar"; it was a restaurant where families and children came. It did have a bar in it, but being the drunk obnoxious guy wasn't going to fare well in a small town like this.

I went back to the table where Jim and a group of our friends were hanging out. Minutes after my interaction with the drunk guy, I looked over to see he was being escorted out, but not by a uniformed officer.

It was a man, dressed in jeans and a plaid shirt, black shiny boots, and perfectly styled sunshine blonde hair. A mystery man I had never seen there before. It was a place I frequented on weekends, so I would have noticed him. He was very handsome. Him taking control of the situation with the drunk guy (who was now trying to remove clothing in public) caught my attention. I watched as he escorted him out and returned to the seat that I had just occupied minutes before. He started talking to my friend, the bartender. It was obvious they knew each other. I figured I'd get the tea on mystery man later when I wasn't out with Jim. He had a jealous streak a mile long and the fact that we weren't together made it worse. After some time, I stepped outside to have a cigarette and took a phone call from my dad.

As I got off the phone, the blue eyed mystery man asked me how my night was going. Everything about him read rookie police officer. The neat spiky hair, the ridiculously shiny boots, the G-Shock watch, even the way he stood. He had to be watching the door, planning his escape route just in case. Just his presence in general read law enforcement. So I asked him point blank, "Where are you a cop?" I laugh at that now but it's a true story. He was in the academy to become a certified police officer. We spent several minutes talking. I told him I wanted to be an officer so I could be promoted to detective one day and help people who had been through tough situations like mine.

Suddenly, Jim appeared and joined the conversation. He made sure to tell this guy I was his "fiance" several times, which wasn't even remotely true. We had been separated for months. Mystery man introduced himself as Eli. I gave Eli my number so he could put me in contact with a recruiter for his police department. I would have given him my phone number anyway because he was HAWT. The big dummy entered my number in his phone wrong. Insert facepalm here. But as luck would have it, Eli must have had the same interest I did because he returned to the same place looking for me the next week. I didn't go on Friday, so he returned on Saturday. I decided to go and take Noah that Saturday night. On the car ride over, I was telling some friends about Eli. As soon as the doors opened, there he sat and we locked eyes. It was just meant to happen that way.

We spent the entire evening talking and hanging out. He even threw me to the ground. That's completely a joke too: I had asked him how to get someone to the ground and as he was showing me, I fell backwards. The looks on people's faces were priceless as they thought I was being assaulted. I had to jump up and explain that I fell.

We ended the evening with Eli walking Noah to the car for me because he was asleep. I assumed Eli wasn't interested in me because we never exchanged numbers. I went home and went about my night. I really wasn't looking for a relationship, or at least not anything serious. I had just gotten out of a bad three year relationship and for once was trying to find my own footing. Just me and Noah. Something about Eli just pulled me to him. Not sure if it was the blue eyes or the grin but there was just something about him.

Chapter 27

The First Date

The next day, I drove to the bartender's house. I wanted the intel on Eli. She had his phone number, but called him to make sure it was ok that she gave his number to me. Of course he said yes. I called and invited him to dinner. My friend practically shoved me out the door so I could meet Eli for dinner, telling me to leave Noah for the night, and to go enjoy dinner.

I rolled my eyes and giggled at her knowing she was trying to play matchmaker, but I took her advice and opted to have an enjoyable evening. I rushed home to change so I wouldn't look like a hot mess and started preparing dinner. Homemade shrimp alfredo was on the menu. Eli arrived right on time. I was still cooking, but he joined me in the kitchen for good conversation until dinner was ready. He made sure to tell me he had to leave by ten. The night carried on with us discussing everything. Likes, dislikes, favorite movies, books, music, our families. If it could be talked about, it was a topic of conversation. The night went perfectly. It was already midnight and Eli should have left two hours earlier, but we were magnets in a sense. We couldn't be pulled apart. I'm not sure if he was nervous or just respecting my boundaries but he was the perfect gentleman. When he did go in for a kiss, it was PERFECT!!!

I really liked Eli, but that also made me nervous. I was really trying not to sabotage myself again and get tied up with another abuser. I was treading so much more carefully than I ever really had. Something about Eli made me feel safe and like I could trust him. I did offer to allow him to stay the night, as it was extremely late. He took me up on my offer. Even though it went against everything I said I wouldn't do, I allowed it. I remember thinking to myself, I'll never hear from him again. He must have sensed what I was thinking because he looked over at that moment and said, "I'm still going to call you tomorrow".

Eli knew I was damaged goods but he didn't seem to care. Maybe it was the officer in him, wanting to "save" me. Whatever it was, it became my safe space. He became my safe space. I truly believe God placed me and Eli in the perfect places at just the perfect times. He made us for each other. After three consecutive date nights in a row, I remember Eli laughing to himself and saying "how is this possible?" I already knew what he was thinking because I felt it too.

I told him it was ok, and that I felt the same way. We were in love. Most would argue that you can't love someone you don't know. I disagree, I loved my children before I knew them. I've loved strangers and showed them love. Sometimes you just know. And I know love at first sight sounds so cliche, but that's exactly what happened. I laid eyes on Eli and that's really where the true story of my healing started. That's not saying that Eli was solely the solution to my healing, but he is the first man I let my guard down with and trusted fully. He taught me to love myself. He looked past the brokenness, even on harder days when it was visible. He listened, let me cry, reassured me when I was unsure, and set out to be a Kintsugi. In every fault I had, he found a solution. I was encouraged during depression and I was held during PTSD flashbacks or anxiety. He became my best friend.

After that day, we were hardly ever separated. Only if we were in class. That's it, we rushed home everyday to be together. Jim wasn't a fan of Eli. In fact, at one point when I met up with Jim to get diapers for Noah, he tried his best to not allow me out of my car and when I told him I was calling Eli, he turned and said I hope he can handle "this." "This" was a knife on his hip in a leather sheath. I laughed in his face and said I hope you can pull that faster than he can pull his trigger. This only made Jim furious. He knew he couldn't live up to the man I had or the relationship we shared.

Not only was Eli amazing to me but he stepped up and became a dad to Noah on day one. I'd have to beg Jim for diapers and Eli would just bring them home. Anything Noah needed, he had between me and Eli. Evenings were spent watching Eli play with Noah and watching what became their bedtime routine. I finally had the family Noah deserved which was all I ever wanted. I knew completely this man either loved me or was crazy when he came and sat in my phlebotomy class. He allowed me to stick him and draw blood nineteen times in two hours. No relationship is perfect but ours was pretty close at that time.

Chapter 28

Mandate Graduation

Eli had successfully completed mandate (the police academy). We dressed in our best and prepared for the day. I was particularly nervous because I was meeting some of his family for the first time. I had met his parents and brother. Now I was meeting the grandparents. The graduation was perfect. Eli received the scholastic award. I was so proud of all his hard work.

At the end of the graduation, the newly graduated officers had to file back into the classroom and be dismissed by their instructors. As Eli was released and started walking towards me, I walked toward him, telling him how proud I was of him. Y'all this man pushed me backwards saying, "Yeah, I'm proud of me too, now shut up."

My fiery redheaded self was about to lose my Jesus when he stopped me in the center of the room, and got down on one knee. I probably sucked up every bit of the oxygen in that room, gasping. I couldn't possibly tell you what he said to me. I have absolutely no idea. I was in such shock, I was looking around at everyone else like "is this really happening?!" It was happening. I, of course, said yes. I was engaged to my best friend. I married my best friend only three months after meeting him.

Chapter 29

Never the Victim

The biggest lesson learned on my journey to healing has been confronting those toxic people who say they love you but the actions don't add up, and ridding them from your presence. The Bible tells us the devil comes to steal, kill, and destroy. Love does not keep score and love does not degrade or belittle you.

For the last fifteen years, I have sat back and put up with far more verbal abuse than I deserved from Stacy. The woman who claims to 'love me.' The woman who will go out of her way to keep score. She makes sure to "remind me" of everything she's done for me. As a mother myself, I cannot keep a tally for every time I've helped or been there for my children. I am their mom, it's my job. I had to learn something recently, she was and is the biggest manipulator and toxic being in my life. She would constantly make comments about my appearance, my hair, my clothes, my weight, anything she could point out, down to belittling me as a mother, as if she was the greatest. To be clear, Stacy worked my entire life so I can't say she didn't support me, but that doesn't give her permission to do irreparable damage to people. She was my "mom" and I "allowed" her to say things to me that were in no way appropriate or things a mother should say, chopping it up to "that's just how mom is." That doesn't make the things she said or did ok. It was her choosing to say and do hurtful things.

It wasn't until my husband and my best friend Courtney pointed out how damaging her words to me were that I started to question things for myself. When I sent a text telling her she was going to respect my boundaries, that her words were damaging my mental health, I was not met with concern or respect. I was met with blaming and condescending apologies. Below you will see the original message I sent Stacy. This was after being called raggedy and being told my husband was going to leave me. I'm not proud of how I handled everything but it's truthful. This was my text to Stacy:

"This is gonna be long, first off I'm 32 years old. I'm well aware of the fact that I mess up and I'm in no way a perfect mom. I fail every day but your criticism doesn't stop. Even my husband and my best friend have made comments about you constantly ragging on me. You cannot "be concerned about my depression" when you help aid in the cause of it. You'd probably know better than anyone that I've had a less than easy life, so piling it on whenever you can doesn't help. Comments about my weight, how I look, and what a crap parent I am do not help me. Frankly, they push me further into my depressive states and away from you. However, you can ask Eli or my best friend, I'm not depressed. I've actually been in a really good place lately besides the fact that my body hurts a lot (but that's health related) and YOU constantly tearing me down. Bringing up my past marital problems with my husband is so uncalled for and so out of line. I leaned on you in a hard time in our marriage and now you use it against me. My marriage works even if you don't see it that way and respectfully, you are the last person that needs to give anyone marital advice. Yes, we fight sometimes .We have a very busy, stressful life with very little time for each other and very little money but overall we are happy. Yes we have made financial mistakes, who doesn't? And yes you have helped us before but that does not give you permission to talk down to me or comment on my home, kids, etc. I don't recall you being the perfect mom or having the easiest time with ███ either. Stop throwing the stones just because you've moved out of your glass house. I seriously don't know why you are constantly on me, but maybe you needed the counseling I got. I'm setting boundaries for myself and my family now. My 3 year old is allowed to be 3 without being told he's a baby for crying. Noah is allowed to embrace who he is without being talked down to, especially by someone who has zero knowledge of how to deal with a child like him. And I am telling you that this constant need to drag everything about me stops now or we won't be visiting and all that any more. You're my mom, you're supposed to support and encourage me not tear me down over mistakes, hard times and problems in my life. I am 100% done with being treated this way. I am a person, I have fought hard as fuck to even have a seemingly normal life and you and your husband will respect it and my boundaries or you can exit just like everyone else has. One thing you did teach me is to stand up for myself, so I'm doing it. Never thought I'd have to do it with you but if you don't believe you've been critical of me, call my husband and ask how he's seen it in the last 10 years. As for tonight, don't bother coming. And I'm not sure we can make it Sunday. We really don't have the gas money a bill came out that I forgot about but that another fuck up by me."

This is where everything gets sort of interesting. It becomes a back and forth. The above text is me telling her I can't deal with any more negativity. This is where the gaslighting starts. I am NOT proud of some of my responses or language. I was at my wit's end and reacted out of anger. I asked to be respected and it took me becoming this ugly person to remove her from my life as well. This was Stacy's response:

"You can set your boundaries if you want but you need to realize that what I say to you is out of love. You are very critical of me as well. I see you struggling with everything and I don't want to see the kids end up in trouble later in life because they lack structure. You can choose to do what you want but remember who has always been there for you no matter what!!!!! I have always had your back!! You are on this kick that you are going to live your life so live it. I see you making some of the same mistakes I did . █████ tried to reach out to you so that he could see if he could help you fix the power situation but you gave him a short answer. It's not fair to let the kids suffer. I will make sure they get their presents even if I have to mail them because I have offended you. The kids are not babies anymore no matter how much you want them to be. You talk to them like a 2 year old wee Wee and Rae Rae. But I will say this everything I said was because I love and care about all of you. Maybe I am not the best at delivering my message and neither are you. I guess I just got put in the █████ category because I tried to give you advice but it is what it is that is a choice that you can make. I love all of you. You are making life hard on yourself by alienating everyone then you complain about not being able to go anywhere people would be willing to help you out more but you are alienating everyone."

That was the response that was met with setting my boundary. It got worse in texts just a few weeks later when I questioned if she took money for my adoption and asked her to acknowledge her ultimatum on the adoption: This was Stacy's response.

I won't apologize for the decision 16 years ago because I didn't feel like it was the best for you to have a molesters baby in your face everyday. I would have had to take on the burden of being the responsibility and I didn't think it was best for you. I was told by Greg that he would leave if I let you have him and stay. Again I am the bad guy because I agreed that I didn't think it was the best for you. It's a decision I made and I won't apologize for it. I did as a mother what I thought was best at the time. I don't have to take responsibility

When confronted with what she said to me, she first blames my dad who passed away in 2021. He is not here to tell his side of the story or answer for anything. He and my mom were divorced at the time of his death. He did ask her to remain as his power of attorney. She didn't help plan his funeral because of her boyfriend at the time. I planned his service, she took the life insurance money she had on him, and moved on with life. She then said that I was not a victim or groomed at all.

Griffin to be with you. That is not grooming that is you being infatuated with a grown man . So why don't you take responsibility for your actions quit acting like you are the sole victim. Your actions affected everyone . Why don't you take a look at yourself you keep saying I need to you run off ███████ with your drama now it's me and ████ you keep alienating people and you are the key person isn't that what you told me last night look in the mirror honey before you blame everybody else you seem to be they key person as well.

Here I am, almost sixteen years later, with more questions than answers because Stacy is a professional at gaslighting, lying, manipulation, and blaming. She has legal documents that belong to me, which she claimed were sent to her. My adopted son's social security card would not have been mailed to her as I was his legal birth mother.

The biggest reason why I began asking questions is because when Rob was sentenced, he was ordered to pay restitution. That happened in 2007. I wasn't notified or aware of it until 2021, when the court system finally found me to inform me that they had been looking for me and of the restitution. He was ordered to pay $4,000. Of that $4,000, I've received $200. When I brought it to her attention, her response was "ugh that was supposed to come to me for the ring and cellphone he took from my house" even though he was never charged with any theft offense and the theft, if it happened, would have occurred 50 miles away in another jurisdiction. There was no concern for the daughter he took. She cared about the money.

When I asked for the legal documents that belong to me, that she claims "she kept to protect me" and I offered to pay for them to be mailed certified, I was told no and to find them for myself. She took zero responsibility for anything she had ever done.

IN THE SUPERIOR COURT OF COBB COUNTY, GEORGIA Filed In Office Nov-12-2007 17:28:58
ID# 2007-████-CR
Page 1

CRIMINAL ACTION NO. 07-████
WARRANT NO. 06-W-█

Jay C. Stephenson
Clerk of Superior Court Cobb County

The State

vs

OFFENSE(S) Ct 1. Agg. Child Molestation
Ct 2 - Statutory Rape
Ct 3 - Statutory Rape
Ct 4 Enticing a Child for indecent purpose

☐ PLEA   ☐ NON-JURY   ☐ JURY   ☐ VERDICT
☑ NEGOTIATED   ☐ GUILTY ON   ☐ OTHER DISPOSITION
☐ GUILTY ON COUNT(S) 2   COUNT(S) _____   ☐ NOLLE PROSEQUI ORDER ON
☐ NOLO CONTENDERE ON   ☐ NOT GUILTY ON   COUNT(S) 1, 3, 4
COUNT(S) _____   COUNT(S) _____   ☐ DEAD DOCKET ORDER ON
☐ TO LESSER INCLUDED   ☐ GUILTY OF LESSER INCLUDED   COUNT(S) _____
ON COUNT(S) _____   ☐ MERGED COUNT(S) _____
OFFENSE(S) _____

☑ FELONY SENTENCE   ☐ MISDEMEANOR SENTENCE

WHEREAS, the above-named defendant has been found guilty of the above-stated offense, WHEREUPON, it is ordered and adjudged by the Court that the said defendant hereby sentenced to confinement for a period of 20 twenty years

In the State Penal System or such other institution as the Commission of the State Department of Corrections or Court may direct, to be computed as provided by law, HOWEVER, it is further ordered by the Court
☐ THAT the above sentence may be served on probation.
☑ THAT upon service of 10 ten years of the above sentence, the remainder of 10 ten years may be served on probation
PROVIDED that the said defendant complies with the following general and other conditions herein imposed by the Court as part of this sentence.

☑ GENERAL AND/OR OTHER CONDITIONS OF PROBATION Sex offender conditions

1) Do not violate the criminal laws of any governmental unit. Register as a sex offender
2) Avoid injurious and vicious habits-especially alcoholic consumption/intoxication and narcotics and other dangerous drugs unless lawfully requesting.
3) Avoid persons or places of disreputable or harmful character.
4) Report to the Probation-Parole Supervisor as directed and permit such Supervisor to visit him (her) at home or elsewhere.
5) Work faithfully at suitable employment insofar as may be possible. no contact with Ashley
6) Do not change his (her) present place of abode, move outside the jurisdiction of the Court, or leave the State for any period of time without prior permission of the Probation Supervisor.
7) Support his (her) dependents to the best of his (her) ability.

10% Jail Surcharge pursuant to O.C.G.A. 15-21-93
32.00 Per Month Probation Fee not to exceed 90 payments
Probation Surcharge pursuant to O.C.G.A. 42-8-34 / 15-21 A-6
10% Brain and Spinal Injury Trust Fund pursuant to O.C.G.A. 15-21-149
50% Drug Surcharge pursuant to O.C.G.A. 15-21-100
IT IS FURTHER ORDERED that the defendant pay a fine in the amount of .... and pay victim restitution in the amount to exceed 750.00 Defendant to pay all fines, penalties and restitution as a condition of probation at the rate of $ 100.00 per month beginning 60 days from release

9% Victim Assistance Surcharge pursuant to O.C.G.A. 15-21-131
OUI Surcharge pursuant to O.C.G.A. 15-21-112
$50 or 10% POPDF whichever is less pursuant to O.C.G.A.15-21-73 (a)(1)(A)
10% POPDF of original fine pursuant to O.C.G.A., 15-21-73 (a)(1)(B)
5% of original fine for GA. Driver's Education Commission pursuant to O.C.G.A. 15-21-179
$100 Court Costs pursuant to O.C.G.A. 15-6-77(6) (7) 4000.00 and

SEE ADDENDUM "A" FOR SPECIAL CONDITIONS OF PROBATION

IT IS THE FURTHER ORDER of the Court, and the defendant is hereby advised that the Court may, at any time, revoke any conditions of this probation and/or discharge the defendant from probation. The probationer shall be subject to arrest for violation of any condition of probation herein granted. If such probation is revoked, the Court may order the execution of the sentence which was originally imposed or any portion thereof in the manner provided by law after deducting therefrom the amount of time the defendant has served on probation.

The defendant was represented by the Honorable Rick Christian Attorney at Law. Cobb County, by (Employment) (Appointment)

Reported By Kim Elias _____ By the Court _____ , 00

So ordered this 12 day of Nov. 2007

Defendant _____   Judge, Cobb Superior Court

IN THE SUPERIOR COURT OF COBB COUNTY

STATE OF GEORGIA

STATE OF GEORGIA   :   INDICTMENT/ACCUSATION

VS.   :   NUMBER: ▮▮▮▮

_____ :

(Defendant)   :

ADDENDUM " _A_ "

SPECIAL CONDITIONS OF PROBATION
FOR
CHILD ABUSER/SEX OFFENDER

PROOF BY A PREPONDERANCE OF EVIDENCE OF A VIOLATION OF ANY OF THE SPECIAL
CONDITIONS CHECKED BELOW WILL AUTHORIZE THE COURT TO REVOKE YOUR
PROBATION AND YOU MAY BE REQUIRED TO SERVE UP TO THE BALANCE OF THE SENTENCE
IN CONFINEMENT AS PROVIDED IN O.C.G.A. 42-8-34.1.

1. Defendant will submit a schedule of weekly activities to the probation officer and will be subject to curfews at the officer's discretion.
2. Defendant will sign a waiver of confidentiality allowing the disclosure of information about this conviction.

Department of Family and Children Services, treatment providers, the Court, and officers of the Court.
3. Defendant will not leave his/her county of residence without the prior knowledge and consent of the probation officer.
4. Defendant will remain appropriately clothed when in public and when the potential for public view exists.
5. Defendant shall undergo an evaluation and all necessary treatment for sexual deviancy, violence, alcohol, and/ or substance abuse in a program approved or designated by the probation supervisor at defendant's own expense.
6. Defendant will continue in treatment and counseling for the duration of this probation unless officially discharged by the probation supervisor and by the court.
7. Defendant is prohibited from working, volunteering, participating in, or having any direct association whatsoever with any day care center or children's programs, including but not limited to programs involving sports, recreation, athletics, education, schools, pre-schools, school buses, school bus stops, Girl Scouts, Boy Scouts, youth choirs, youth programs, YMCA, YWCA, and any other volunteer program, activity or community service work involving direct contact with children under the age of 18.
8. Defendant shall not linger or stop at any middle, elementary, or high schools nor at any school bus stops, amusement parks, playgrounds, and arcades.
9. Defendant shall not initiate contact with nor continue uninitiated contact with a child under the age of 18.
10. Defendant shall not be in the presence of a child under the age of 18 without the immediate presence of the supervisor who has been approved by the treatment provider and probation officer.
11. Defendant is to have absolutely no direct or indirect contact whatsoever, of any kind, with the victims(s) and witnesses or their families, including _Ashley ▮▮▮▮ and her minor child,_

Defendant shall not write, telephone, e-mail, visit, send messages to, speak with, have any computer contact with, or have any contact whatsoever with the above persons.
12. Defendant shall pay restitution for costs and expenses of therapy and counseling for the victim in an amount not to exceed $4,000.00 pursuant to receipts furnished by the victim to the probation officer.
13. Defendant is to submit to an HIV test.
14. Defendant is to be supervised the entire period of his/her probation for the purpose of protecting children.
15. Defendant shall not reside in a home where persons under 18 years of age, reside without the prior knowledge and consent of the probation supervisor, district attorney's office, and the court.

As you can see highlighted in the sentencing above, Stacy was not ordered any sort of restitution in this case as she wasn't the victim in this case. I would have never known about the restitution had the court system not found me and she would have never said a word. Money was her motive. Oh, and her need to "protect me from things I couldn't handle" (like me finding out that money was ordered to me and not her). What she fails to realize is that $200 I've received doesn't give back anything I've sacrificed or experienced. Unfortunately, I had to go on a hunting expedition to find these legal documents, since they have purposefully been withheld from me since 2007.

I could produce a book alone of the "incriminating" evidence of text messages she has sent me, but you get the point. All of this made me realize that I was holding on to the one "parent" I had for the sake of having one, even if she wasn't healthy for me. I have settled for less than I deserve, especially as an adult. The final straw for me was her telling me "she wasn't going to raise a supposed rapist's baby." She says this repeatedly in both texts and I also have it in recorded phone calls. If she truly thinks I wasn't a victim of my own story, then concocting a master plan to inform my entire family that "the adoption was solely my choice and not to ask me about it because it was a sensitive subject" wouldn't have taken place and she wouldn't have put me through years of counseling.

After talking to most members of my family, I found out that they never asked me because Stacy asked them not to bring it up. Leaving me to believe I was alone. Meanwhile, she was just moving her pieces to fit her narrative. Point blank, carrying a child doesn't make you a mother if you lack the capacity to actually be one.

The same goes for Stan. Neither one of them are real parents and truly lack the knowhow to be one. She goes even further to insinuate that I have mental health issues by texting my husband in the message below, when she gets questioned on these matters.

(No subject)

I guess Ashley has chosen to cut me off for trying to protect her and blaming me for everything but I only did what I thought was best for her mental health regardless of what she said she was not ok at that time and Greg refused to have a rapist baby under his roof. Financially I could not afford to pay for everything because I had just basically spent everything I had to find her. Everything thing I did was out of love and protection for her but I guess now she feels that it was my fault. I never hid anything from her the only reason I had paperwork was for the courts. I think she is having an issue with her decision but she was in counseling and seeing Lucy at the pregnancy center so if she wanted the baby she could have worked it out at that time she made it clear that it was her decision. I guess she doesn't remember that but if she wants to be mad at someone she should be mad at ━━━━━━ who created this whole situation. Instead she will speak to him on the phone and meet him but now I am the bad guy. When is she going to take responsibility for her actions she snuck around for weeks meeting him and left with him willingly. She made the choice to go with him not me so it was not my responsibility to raise a child because she was not capable of doing it mentally or physically. I love you all and please take care of her she has blocked me so I guess she has cut me out of her life for protecting her. I am worried that she is headed for a crash and burn so please take care of her. I love you all.

Chapter 30

ALWAYS THE VICTOR

Today, I stand stronger than ever prepared to tell MY story. I'm not letting others write that narrative for me any longer. I am not allowing Stacy or Stan to control me. I have lived in those shadows for far too long. God has moved a lioness in me that is both embracing that scared teenage girl and also protecting her today. I didn't go through hell and forge those fires to let everyone tear down who I am today.

I am facing each day with love in my heart and with a passion to help those beat their odds. Sexual assault doesn't define me. Bad choices do not deem me unworthy. Mistakes to not make me less than, and those that tried to tear me down do not get to decide how long I stay down. I am up by God's grace and I am swinging

I AM THE VICTOR.

Social Media

Website: www.alwaysthevictors.com

Email: alwaysthevictor@yahoo.com

Tiktok: @alwaysthevictor938

Facebook: Always the Victor

IG: alwaysthevictor938

www.ingramcontent.com/pod-product-compliance
Lightning Source LLC
Chambersburg PA
CBHW052130270326
41930CB00012B/2828